Other books by Iyanla Vanzant

Acts of Faith
The Value in the Valley
Faith in the Valley
One Day My Soul Just Opened Up
In the Meantime
Don't Give It Away!
Yesterday, I Cried
Until Today!

living through the MEANTIME

*learning to break the patterns of the past
and begin the healing process*

IYANLA VANZANT

A FIRESIDE BOOK
Published by Simon & Schuster
New York   London   Toronto   Sydney   Singapore

FIRESIDE
Rockefeller Center
1230 Avenue of the Americas
New York, NY 10020

Copyright © 2001 by Inner Visions Worldwide Network, Inc.
All rights reserved,
including the right of reproduction
in whole or in part in any form.

FIRESIDE and colophon are registered trademarks
of Simon & Schuster, Inc.

Designed by Bonni Leon-Berman

Manufactured in the United States of America

3   5   7   9   10   8   6   4

Library of Congress Cataloging-in-Publication Data is available.

ISBN 0-7432-2710-7
For information regarding special discounts for bulk purchases,
please contact Simon & Schuster Special Sales at
1-800-456-6798 or business@simonandschuster.com

ACKNOWLEDGMENTS

I acknowledge God, by all the names S/He is known as the Source and center of my life, for the good I have done and become.

I acknowledge and humbly thank Obatala and Osun as the divine expressions of God that chose to express through me.

I acknowledge YOU! For your willingness to grow and your willingness to know the truth about you, about life and about the Source.

I acknowledge and humbly thank the staff, students and supporters of Inner Visions Worldwide Network for their tireless support and efforts that have kept the ministry afloat and made all the work worthwhile.

I acknowledge and humbly thank my offspring, Damon Keith, Gemmia Lynnette, Nisa Camille, and my surrogate offspring J. Alexander Morgan for never once complaining about all the years they spent in the *meantime* with me.

I acknowledge chocolate cake, Häagen-Dazs coffee ice cream, Folgers coffee, and smoked turkey on a croissant as being among the greatest joys one can have in a meantime experience.

I acknowledge and humbly thank the love of my life, Adeyemi Bandele, for being my "Pumpkin."

CONTENTS

ENTERING THE MEANTIME

YOU'VE GOT TO CLEAN THE HOUSE
BEFORE YOU CAN LIVE IN IT!

welcome! Chances are, if you have put forth the effort and energy to find this book, you are in the *"meantime."* I welcome you because I know something wonderful is about to happen—in your life and for you.

You probably think your life or some part of it is falling apart. The truth of the matter is everything is about to come together just the way you have always wanted it to!

The objective of this *meantime* workbook is to help you put the pieces of your life together—the missing pieces, the broken pieces, the confusing pieces, and the lost pieces. We are going to go through every inch of your emotional and spiritual house and clean up the mess, clear out the debris, fix the leaks, stop the squeaks, and reveal and repair any damage we can find. This workbook is designed to support you while you do the work required to build a solid structure that is grounded in love. Let me warn you right now, it may not be easy! But then, you knew that, didn't you?

ARE YOU READY TO WORK?

The *meantime* is a working time. It is the 9–5 of your life to which you bring all that you have studied, learned, been told, understand, and recognize about yourself and life. The *meantime* is a time of strengthening that knowledge so that it can work through you and for you. The *meantime* is where you land when you saw it coming, did not know what to do about it, ran around frantically for a while, and finally said, "Okay! Okay! I don't like it, but I am willing to deal with it!" Willingness is the key that transforms a character-developing experience into a soul-enhancing one. At the core of your soul is the essence of love.

In the *meantime,* you get to deal with all the pieces of your experience that you do not like, but are at least willing to understand. Understanding is the ticket through the *meantime.* Every step or misstep you have ever taken has led to this moment. You are exactly where you need to be, doing exactly what you need to be doing in order to move into a higher consciousness. This is the place you had to come to in order to "bump" your life up to the next level. The *meantime* is about pumping up the volume— the volume of love you are willing to give and receive.

In the midst of the *meantime,* it may *appear* that you are standing on shaky ground. The truth is you are standing on *Holy Ground.* Oh by the way, did I mention that the *meantime* is grounded in truth? The truth of who you are, the truth about what you do, the truth about what you want, the truth about what you see, the truth about what you know, and the truth about what you do not know. Furthermore, in the midst of the *meantime* experience, there is the truth about your ability to recognize each of these, and it is *this truth* that ultimately determines how you make it through whatever you are going through.

In the *meantime*, you are engaged in a Holy Healing process which your soul signed up for because, at the deepest level of your soul, you know that love is the only way to get what you really want. In the *meantime*, you will have to work through your stuff.

WHERE IS THE MESS?

A feeling is the energy that moves you in one direction or another. If you get stuck in a feeling, you won't move in any direction at all. What you are *feeling* determines the kind of work you must do to make it through the *meantime*. The following is a basic guideline you can use to figure out where you live.

you are doing basement work if you are feeling disappointed, betrayed, rejected, and/or like where you are is someone's fault. You've got a problem, but you don't know it.

you are doing first-floor work if you are feeling angry, frightened, confused, unhappy, and/or apprehensive, or believe your life is falling apart. You've got a problem, but you don't know what it is.

you are doing second-floor work if you are ending a relationship that you don't want to end, leaving employment that you didn't have the courage to leave, going back to school, moving to a new location just to get away from the old one, opening a business because you got kicked out of your job, and/or facing a serious health challenge because of lack of self-care. You've got a problem, you know what it is, but you don't know what to do about it.

you are stuck between the second and third floors if you are asking Why me??? Why now??? Why should I??? How come??? How can I??? When will it end??? When will it begin??? What the heck is going on??? You've got a problem, you know what it is, you know what to do about it, but you are afraid to do it.

you are doing third-floor work if you are seeking closure to dysfunctional relationships, ready to forgive people you've been in relationships with, ready to forgive yourself for staying in relationships and situations you knew you had no business being in, and/or you are ready to assume full responsibility for every aspect of your life. You don't have problems. You have challenges, and you feel perfectly equipped to handle them.

you are doing attic work if you are feeling or saying I am grateful! I am hopeful! I am ready! I am open!

MAKE SURE YOU'RE IN THE RIGHT HOUSE!!!

Just to be on the safe side, let's take a quick inventory to make sure that this is the book you need.

You are in the *meantime* if:

💜 You are confused, angry, disappointed, frustrated about something that has happened in your life.

💜 You have just been fired, left, divorced, had surgery, or been released from prison.

💜 You feel anxious, apprehensive, beat up, beat down, sorry for yourself, unhappy with yourself, numb, or generally wiped out.

If, however, you are in rage, depression, seeking vengeance or revenge; if you are seeing red, black, or green at the thought of a particular person or situation, **you are not in the *meantime*.** You are in a valley!

A valley experience is very different from a *meantime* situation. When you are in a valley, you are having an experience that fosters character development. When you find yourself in a valley, it is because you have missed the boat! You have displayed either an inability or an unwillingness to examine and accept the truth about yourself. You are learning a lesson that you missed because you insisted on *"having it your way"* or *"doing your thing,"* even when you knew that your way would not work. If you are in a valley you are probably crying in anger, breaking dishes, talking really badly about someone, and being a victim—again! You probably sound something like this, "I gave my all and got messed over—again!" Or, "I bent over backwards trying to do it right, only to be overlooked, left, mistreated—again!"

If you find yourself in a miserable experience you swore you would never be in again, chances are you didn't see it coming. Not because you couldn't see it, but because you didn't want to see it.

Now that what you saw and refused to accept has bitten you on the butt, you are really, really, really pissed off! It's called *pissosity!* That is the state in which most valley dwellers find themselves before they become aware that there is work to be done. They are either comatose or in a highly agitated state of *pissosity.*

If this clearly or closely describes your current state of being, I humbly suggest that you go back and read *The Value in the Valley: A Black Woman's Guide Through Life's Dilemmas.* Do not get hung up on the fact that you may not be black or that you may not be a woman. Read it anyway! I can almost guarantee that there is something you need to know about yourself in the pages of that book.

If you are actually in a valley, you may find there is a little help for you in this workbook; however, you must be *willing* to do the work required. This means no more blaming. Blaming is pointing *out there,* rather than *in here,* into your own mind, when you find yourself in a painful or uncomfortable experience. Blame means shifting the responsibility for where you are onto someone or something else, rather than accepting responsibility for your role in the experience.

A *meantime* experience is a very different experience. When you are in the *meantime,* you are hurt, but you are not blaming anyone else unless you are in the basement. You will know you are in the basement if you are ready to feel better by any means necessary. You are angry, but you are willing to forgive, even if forgiving means acknowledging that *you made a mistake,* a poor choice, or a big boo-boo. You are confused, but you have not pulled the covers up over your head, refusing to come out until someone or something has its head ripped off.

If you are able to show even the slightest degree of willingness to work on yourself, you may find solace in these pages. Oth-

16

erwise, until you become *willing* to work through some of the anger, pissosity, and blaming, you are going to find that it is very hard to do the healing work required. But, I will leave it up to you to decide where you are and where you want to be.

YOU ARE GOING TO LOVE YOUR NEW HOUSE!

In the *meantime,* you are asking: *What?* What can I do? What did I do? What should I do? What am I learning? You are asking: *How?* How can I stop this cycle? How did I get here? How come . . . ? You are asking: *Why?* Why am I here? Why is this happening? Why this? Why now? This is a very different scenario from the valley scenario. When you are in the valley, the only thing you are asking is *"Why me?!"* You are also placing more emphasis on the *me,* as opposed to the *why.* This is precisely why the *meantime* is a very different experience. You have come to the *meantime* to evolve, not to develop; to get clear, not to find your eyes! More specifically, you have come to the *meantime* to learn about love.

Love does not hurt. It gently guides you to where you need to be at any given time in your life. Love is not out to crush you. Love opens your eyes, clears your mind, and above all, opens your heart to a greater experience of yourself. Now, I will admit that there are those situations when it *appears* that love has left you high and dry on the desert, without so much as a thimbleful of water. That is, however, just an appearance. Things are rarely as they appear to be, and the purpose of a *meantime* experience is to move you beyond appearances to the true essence of you: love.

If you are not giving and receiving love in all of your life's experiences, you will find yourself in one *meantime* experience after another. To move from one level of consciousness to another, from one level of self-awareness to another, you must be

17

grounded in love, you must engage in loving behavior. In this workbook, you will repeatedly be asked if you have engaged in loving behavior, or if you have acted out a habitual thought pattern, such as fear, greed, or the most common of human behaviors, unconsciousness. Under all circumstances, life expects us to behave in a loving manner, whether we are conscious or not. I hope the work you will do in this book will support you in maintaining a loving consciousness.

LOVING BEHAVIOR REFERENCE

For reference, whether you make it through the work in this book or not, the most loving way you can behave through any experience is:

- Ask for exactly what you want.
- Tell the absolute truth about what you want.
- Clearly let others involved know your expectations of them.
- Ask for clarity about what is expected of you.
- Tell the absolute truth about your ability to live up to the expectations of others.
- Renegotiate any agreements you have made if you find that you're unable to keep the agreement.
- Honor what you feel, first to yourself, then to others around you.
- Remain open to hearing what others want and expect without feeling you have to do anything about it.
- Never dishonor or deny yourself or what you feel simply to please someone else.

♥ Be willing to surrender (give up) what you want or expect when surrendering it serves a greater purpose, such as healing or generating more love.

♥ Be willing to forgive people for the things they do or fail to do in fear or anger.

♥ Be willing to forgive yourself for the things you do in fear or in anger.

♥ Bless every experience and ask that Divine will and understanding be granted to you and others.

ROLL UP YOUR SLEEVES!

This workbook is designed to support you as you examine and explore the situations that brought you to the *meantime* experience. At first, some topics may seem to have no relevance to your situation or experience. **TRUST THE PROCESS!** All is relevant, and as you go through the process, all you need to know will be revealed.

The idea behind *meantime* work is to *save yourself* from having the same *meantime* experience in the future. Something you are thinking, believing, saying, or doing is taking you away from your heart's desire. Our goal is to get to the heart of the matter in order to find love that you can give away, in order to receive. Your objective is to identify the contributing elements of your *meantime* situation and break them down into bite-size pieces that you can ingest and digest. You will do a great deal of writing so that you can get clear and be clear before you make another move or give birth to more of what you do not want to experience.

There are a few things you can do to make your healing process more effective in the *meantime:*

FORGIVE YOURSELF!

You have never done anything wrong. Now you can forgive yourself for ever believing that you did. Oh by the way, everyone else you have ever encountered is as innocent of wrongdoing as you are! (Take a breath! You will understand what I mean later.)

TRUST YOURSELF!

Because you are a unique and divine expression of God (known by whatever name you are comfortable with), you are worthy and can be trusted, because you really know what to do.

SUPPORT YOURSELF!

You deserve a kind word, a good thought, a loving gesture every now and then, so give them to yourself!

HONOR YOURSELF!

Stop criticizing, judging, denying, and second guessing what you feel and who you are!

FORTIFY YOURSELF!

Get lots of rest. Eat good healthy foods! Spend some quiet time alone with *you*. And, don't forget to have some fun! Playing is a big part of a good life.

COMMIT YOURSELF!

Take some part of each day and use it to take one step toward accomplishing a daily, weekly, or monthly goal!

LOVE YOURSELF!

You are the one that the world is waiting for! You are so precious to life, you must make it a high priority to let *you* know that you are loved, needed, and wanted by God!

YOU'LL NEED A BROOM

This workbook is a healing process designed to help you remember what you forgot; become conscious of the things you may not now be conscious of; and to get to know parts of yourself that you don't know. To accomplish any or all of this is a process!!! Do not try to rush through this book. You will fall! You will crash! Healing takes time, so feel free to take as much time as you need to complete the work in this book.

You may find it is easier to use a notebook or journal to do the actual work. In this way you can reuse a particular page as often as you feel it's necessary. Please feel free to do and redo the same worksheet as many times as necessary to get to higher ground, a deeper feeling of peace, or to gain more clarity. As you are writing, honor what you feel.

Your feelings are the keys you need to unlock the mystery of your *meantime* experience. If at any time, whether you are doing a worksheet or not, you become overwhelmed by a need to express what you are feeling, you can use your journal to vent, capture, cleanse, and heal the experience. Whether you are angry, sad, excited, happy, confused, frustrated, or highly pissed off, you must vent. It is good for the soul. Venting also helps you to get clear about what you are feeling in the privacy of your own mind before you bite someone else's head off!

It is also advisable to use a pencil rather than a pen, because as you get clear, you may need to add or subtract from your response. Know that whatever you decide to do is fine.

NICE AND EASY IS MORE THAN HAIR DYE!!!

To complete one exercise a day is wonderful. It would be even better if you complete one every three or four days. In this way you give your mind and soul the opportunity to integrate and heal whatever you may discover or uncover.

You may work through the book in any manner you choose. You may follow the order of the book, doing one exercise at a time. You may zero in on one issue or a particular area, and complete that work first. You may just open the book and begin working in a particular section. You have many, many options. If, however, at any time you are working in this book and find that you feel afraid, overwhelmed, or that your mind has gone blank, STOP! Take a few deep breaths. Stretch your body and take a drink of water before you go any further.

BREATHE!!!

I hope that in the process of working through this book, you will have many revelations. You may realize that things you have done have not been in your best interest. When this happens, you may be overwhelmed with the feeling that you have *"done it wrong."* If or when this happens, take a breath. Take a long, deep breath! You are not nor have you ever been wrong. You may have been unconscious at a particular moment, but you are never wrong! Remember, where you are is exactly where you need to be in order to get to where you want to go. Breathing deeply and releasing fear will help you get to where you want to be.

If at any time when you are working in this book, you feel that you cannot breathe or that your breathing has become labored, STOP! Close the book. Take a nice hot bath or shower. You can try again at another time. Your body knows how much you can do. Do not push yourself. That is not a very loving thing to do when you are healing.

Before you begin any exercise, be sure you have adequate time to complete an entire process. Select a time and place where you will not be disturbed. You may want to take a relaxing bath first. It may also be helpful to have some soothing music playing. Also, give yourself permission to participate fully in this process and experience whatever comes up for you. If you feel the need to stomp, scream, cry, laugh, or throw something *unbreakable*—GO FOR IT! You are safe! You are allowed! Just remember to breathe. Love is always around you. Breathing allows you to take in as much love as you need.

DON'T FORGET TO TAKE CARE OF YOURSELF!

Each section of the workbook also provides a **Caring Exercise** to be used *before you begin* and *when you end* a workbook exercise. The purpose of caring for yourself before and after an exercise is to avoid the possibility of *drowning* in a sea of fear, anger, or confusion. It is necessary so that you do not become overwhelmed by the information that is revealed as you move through the workbook pages. The purpose of caring for yourself at the end of an exercise is to support the integration of what you discover, remember, or realize in the process. Beginning and ending with the Caring Exercise is a good way to coordinate your healing steps with the day-to-day activity of your life.

There is also a **Glossary** at the back of the book. The purpose of the glossary is to assist you in understanding what you are working *with*, what you are working *through*, and what you are working *toward*. If you are not clear about how you can transform your choices or approaches to a particular situation, the glossary will help you make a loving choice.

BEHOLD! YOU WILL DO A NEW THING!!!

On some pages, you will be asked to write with your nondominant hand. This means, if you are right-handed, you will write with your left hand. If you are left-handed, you will write with your right hand. The purpose of this is to reprogram the conscious mind about the issue you are healing. Completing these particular exercises will require focus and energy. The greater the energy you put forth, the greater the healing that will occur. Do not get hung up about what the writing looks like or whether or not you can read it. This is not an art project! It is a healing process. Healing requires focused energy and effort.

"NOW WHERE DID I PUT . . . ? "

You may find throughout the process that there is something you want to write, but you simply can't find the words. At these times, you will find it helpful to stimulate the **Trigger Points** of the brain.

1. If you are right-handed, gently place your second and third fingers over the center of your left eyebrow. Place your thumb over your right eyebrow. If you are left-handed, place your second and third fingers over your right eyebrow. Place your thumb over your left eyebrow.

2. Gently massage these areas for about thirty seconds while thinking about what you truthfully want to write.

3. If you find that the words still do not pop into your mind, use the list of trigger words on the following page to support your description and experience.

positive triggers

Accessible	Creative	Inviting	Self-reliant
Affectionate	Daring	Kind	Sensitive
Agreeable	Debonaire	Lighthearted	Serene
Alert	Dependable	Loving	Sexy
Assured	Determined	Loyal	Sincere
Attentive	Enthusiastic	Mature	Soothing
Available	Fair	Objective	Spiritual
Bold	Firm	Open	Spontaneous
Brave	Flexible	Open-minded	Stable
Bright	Frank	Persuasive	Strong
Calm	Gallant	Playful	Sunny
Caring	Gentle	Pleased	Supportive
Cautious	Giving	Polite	Tactful
Certain	Glad	Precise	Tender
Cheerful	Grateful	Proud	Thrifty
Cheery	High-spirited	Reassuring	Tolerant
Concerned	Hilarious	Reliable	Tranquil
Confident	Honest	Respectful	Trusting
Connected	Humble	Responsible	Virtuous
Content	Independent	Safe	Vivacious
Cordial	Inquisitive	Satisfied	Warm
Courageous	Inspired	Secure	Wise

negative triggers

Afraid	Impatient
Annoyed	Inappropriate
Arrogant	Inflexible
Attacking	Intrusive
Boring	Irrational
Brash	Jealous
Brutal	Judgmental
Cold	Malicious
Complacent	Mean
Controlling	Narrow-minded
Cruel	Rigid
Dangerous	Rough
Depressed	Shy
Dishonest	Sneaky
Disinterested	Stingy
Envious	Strict
Fearful	Tense
Fragile	Tolerable
Frightened	Unavailable
Frightening	Unemotional
Grumpy	Unforgiving
Harsh	Unreliable
Immature	Wounding

just a prayer away!

If at any time you need support, or guidance in the form of prayer, 24-hour help is available to you. The following nondenominational prayer services have staff available to hear your concerns and to pray with you. (These are not counseling services, they are prayer services.) When you reach out to these services, someone will pray with you regarding a challenge you may be experiencing. Prayer changes things! As you pray and are prayed for, things will change for you.

World Ministry of Prayer
(800) 421-9600

Silent Unity
(816) 969-2000

Inner Visions
(301) 608-8750
If you get a recording, press 1 for the Prayer Line.

IF YOU MADE IT THROUGH THE PAST, YOU PASSED!

This workbook is not meant to be the end-all, do-all for you. It is designed to support you in identifying the things you do that could be done in a more loving way. Do not assume, even if you are in the *meantime*, that you are worse off than anyone else. There may be some exercises you may not immediately relate to. There may be some questions that seem totally irrelevant. That's fine! This workbook is designed to make you think and to simplify the process of making better choices in your life in general and in relationships specifically. By the end of the process, you will realize you are the Beloved. Throughout the process, you will get clear about who the Beloved is and what the Beloved does. As you move into a greater awareness of yourself, by acknowledging what you do and accepting yourself just as you are without judgment or criticism, a more loving state of mind unfolds in you and the Beloved comes into full view.

I wish for you loving days, loving experiences, and a loving state of mind. You are the Beloved and all that you are, I AM!

THE BASEMENT

if i were to ask you to make a list of all the low-down, no good, dirty, rotten, wicked people you have met in your life, how long would the list be? If I were to ask you to identify how many times you've been hurt, wronged, used, abused, left high and dry, how much time would it take? Guess what? I'm not going to ask any of that. As of today none of that matters any more! Today you will begin to realize that the only relationship that matters is the one you have with you. Today you will begin building a new, improved relationship. So put the dolls and the pins away.

On each of the worksheets that follow, you will be asked a series of questions designed to support you in becoming conscious of habitual thought patterns, emotions, experiences, and beliefs that may be standing between you and the experience or expression of love. There is no "right" answer to any question. The key is to answer every question as honestly as you possibly can. This usually means responding with the first thought that comes to mind. Your first thought is most often your truest thought.

Be sure to complete the **Caring Exercise** before you begin any section. Once you have completed the section, feel free to reread your responses and jot down any additional thoughts or feelings you may have. When you feel complete, meaning nothing else comes to mind, do the **Closing Caring Exercise.** You may find it helpful to make a copy of a page before you begin, or use a notebook. In that way, you can repeat any exercise as often as you like to gain clarity and closure.

I wish you love!

caring exercise

Before beginning any section of the workbook, please care for yourself. Read each of the following statements silently and then repeat each of the statements aloud. Your words have power! Words create environment and experience. You are free to substitute for "God" any word that makes you comfortable.

I now allow myself to be in the presence of God's love.

I now give myself permission to feel the presence of God's love.

I now open my heart and mind to the healing power of God's love.

I now place my faith in the power and presence of God's love.

I now accept and affirm there is nothing I have done, can do, will do or experience that can separate me from God's love.

I now offer God's love to myself and extend it to everyone involved in my experience of life.

I am grateful that God's love is revealing itself to me.

If you are not giving and receiving love in all of your life's experiences, you will find yourself in one meantime *experience after another. To move from one level of consciousness to another, from one level of self-awareness to another, you must be grounded in love, you must engage in loving behavior.* **You've got to—COORDINATE!**

Clean

Out

Old

Rigid

Destructive

Ideas

Now

And

Truthfully

Evaluate your beliefs

about life and love.

YOU'VE GOT TO LOOK YOURSELF SQUARE IN THE EYE!

Because *I know myself,* I know that *you are probably asking,* "Well, what if I have a combination of responses? Suppose I am disappointed and betrayed because of what someone has done, but I want to find my purpose?" In order to make it through the *meantime* with a minimum amount of confusion, you must: *Coordinate*.

A *meantime* experience is your divine opportunity to coordinate your consciousness, in order to make better, more conscious choices. How is this accomplished? You must call up the Triple A's:

A*wareness*

What is it that you do when you are in fear, anger, anxiety, doubt, under pressure, or in la-la land?

A*cknowledgment*

Once you realize what you do, don't say that you do not do it, or make excuses for why you do it. You can make a conscious choice to change your responses and change the outcome of any situation.

A*cceptance*

Learn to accept what you do as a valuable part of your learning experience and decide whether it is the best way to get what you say you want.

AWARENESS COORDINATION

Think about a recent situation to which you responded in **anger.** What did you do? (If you are not sure, check the Loving Behavior Reference list on **page 18.**)

Were you able to acknowledge to yourself that you were operating in anger? How did you do it?

Were you able to acknowledge to the others involved that you were operating in anger? What did you do / say? If not, why?

ACKNOWLEDGMENT COORDINATION

Complete each of the following sentences after you have revisited your responses on **pages 34–35.**

I am now aware that when I am angry I am prone to

Which makes me feel

The next time I am angry, I can choose to

In this way I will avoid

AWARENESS COORDINATION

Think about a recent situation to which you responded in **fear.**
What did you do? (If you are not sure, check the Loving Behavior
Reference list on **page 18.**)

Were you able to acknowledge to yourself that you were afraid?
How did you do it?

Were you able to acknowledge to the others involved that you were afraid? What did you do/say? If not, why?

ACKNOWLEDGMENT COORDINATION

Complete each of the following sentences after revisiting your responses on **pages 36–37.**

I am now aware that when I am afraid I am prone to

Which makes me feel

The next time I am afraid, I can choose to

In this way I will avoid

You can choose how you will respond to all experiences. Even the good ones. You can only respond with greater consciousness, however, once you become *aware, acknowledge,* and *accept* what you do when you are unconscious. Ninety-percent of the time, it is not the *actual event* that causes our upsets. It is our *response to the event.* This does not mean that a particular response is bad or wrong. Nor does it mean that there are not some pretty difficult experiences to live through. Death of a loved one or a critical illness are two difficult experiences that come to mind. Our goal is to determine whether a particular response is grounded in fear or grounded in love. A fear-based response causes pain, while a love-based response leads to freedom, better choices, and an enhanced state of consciousness. Understanding the Triple A's helps us to choose love- rather than fear-based responses.

HOW DID ALL THIS MESS GET HERE?

In addition to your fear-based responses you must become aware of and acknowledge your unconscious habitual responses. These responses are usually learned. They reflect what you saw those around you do. Habitual responses are so much a part of who you are, and what you do, you probably do not recognize them as the very things that keep you from getting the love you want.

Fear, anger, misinterpretation of your experiences and your

personal judgments of others are the foundation of most of the challenges you face in life. Nothing contributes to these seemingly unfortunate occurrences more than your own unconscious responses—the way you do the things you do. These are things you are consciously not aware that you do.

The ability to recognize unconscious responses provides the opportunity to make better choices. Understanding these responses will also provide answers to the, "What did I do?" and the "Why did this happen to me?" questions. Remember, no response is intrinsically bad or wrong. Keep in mind that the objective of healing work is to facilitate awareness and acceptance of what it is that you do.

DO NOT MESS WITH THE MESS!

Fighting is a fear-based response to an unpleasant experience. Some typical fight responses are:

💜 You hear what is going on in your head, rather than what the person is saying. This usually means you hear something that was not said and try to convince the person that this is what s/he is really saying. Actually, you are responding to *what you think* the person thinks about you. This always leads to a fight!

💜 You challenge the person's right, authority, or intellectual ability to say or do what they are saying or doing. *You think* that s/he thinks that s/he is better, smarter, more something than you are, and you've been dying to tell them off anyway. When you do not say what you need to say when you need to say it, fighting is inevitable.

💜 You believe that survival is an issue, and that your survival is dependent upon a person or a situation. When survival is an issue, you are going to *fight* to stay alive.

💜 If you are a control freak, you will fight at the slightest indication that you are losing control of a person or a situation.

Think of a recent situation in your life where you felt compelled to fight or to defend yourself. What did you do? (If you are not sure, check the Loving Behavior Reference list on **page 18.**)

How did your response make you feel?

ACKNOWLEDGMENT COORDINATION

Complete each of the following sentences after revisiting your responses above.

I am now aware that the way I fight is to

Which makes me feel

The next time I want to fight, I can choose to

In this way I will avoid

DO NOT RUN AWAY FROM THE MESS

To run away is to flee, to avoid, to put off an unpleasant situation until an undetermined time in the not-so-near future. Some of the more common flee responses are:

💜 To never have time to deal with something you know you must deal with.
💜 To make excuses for not dealing with something you know you must eventually deal with.
💜 To see something and call it something else. This is also known as refusal to *call a thing a thing!* In other words, denial!

💜 To see something, know what it is, and ask someone else for an opinion. When the opinion is different from what you know that you know, you accept it anyway. When the opinion is the same as what you know that you know, you ask someone else.

Think of a recent situation in your life that you felt compelled to flee from or avoid. (If you are not sure, check the Loving Behavior Reference list on **page 18.**)

How did your response make you feel?

ACKNOWLEDGMENT COORDINATION

Complete each of the following sentences using the answers you have indicated above.

I am now aware that the way I flee is to

Which makes me feel

The next time I want to flee, I can choose to

In this way I will avoid

DO NOT HIDE FROM THE MESS!

Hiding is another very common fear-based response. It differs from fleeing, because when you hide, you refuse to be found. Some common hiding responses are:

💜 Eating, sleeping, watching television, working at or until an ungodly hour, all of the time.
💜 Refusing to answer the telephone or using caller ID to pick and choose who you will talk to when you are not engaged in some other conscious or productive activity.

♥ Being sick, upset, depressed, angry all of the time without making an effort to figure out why.

When you do not want to deal with an unpleasant or uncomfortable situation, how do you hide?

ACKNOWLEDGMENT COORDINATION

Complete each of the following sentences using the responses you have indicated above.

I am now aware that the way I hide is to

Which makes me feel

The next time I want to hide, I can choose to

In this way I will avoid

DO NOT LIE DOWN AND BURY YOURSELF IN THE MESS!

This is commonly called "submission." Submission is the fear-based response that occurs when you do not have the courage, strength, stamina, or presence of mind to say what you think, talk about how you feel, or ask for what you want. You will also submit when you fear authority or you believe your survival is at stake. Here's what submission can look like:

💜 You determine what a person wants from you, or what the situation demands of you, and give in, even though it makes you sick to your stomach.

💜 You have an opinion, desire, need, or idea, but you do not express it to avoid confrontation.

💜 You have an opinion, desire, need, or idea, but you do not think it's right, or that anyone else agrees with you. In essence, you deny your truth.

💜 You don't say anything to anyone because you are trying to be nice.

💜 You don't say anything to anyone because you want to avoid criticism.

Under what conditions do you feel most compelled to submit to the will of another or the conditions of the environment?

When you submit, what do you do?

When you submit, how does it make you feel?

ACKNOWLEDGMENT COORDINATION

Complete each of the following sentences using the responses you have indicated above.

I am now aware that the way I submit is to

Which makes me feel

The next time I want to submit, I can choose to

In this way I will avoid

DO NOT ATTACK THE MESS!

Attack is a sure sign that you are scared out of your right mind! Attack differs from fighting in that when you attack, what you do or say makes absolutely no sense—not even to you. Your response to a situation is totally out of proportion to its seriousness. When you are attacking:

💜 You make insulting, disparaging, demeaning comments about a person's physical characteristics, intellect, or mother.
💜 You swear, scream, throw things, or make threats of physical harm.

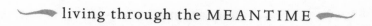

💜 You actually cause physical harm.

💜 You threaten to cause physical harm to yourself.

💜 You play the "Look what you did!" or the "So-and-so did it too!" game.

💜 You call your lawyer or threaten to call your lawyer.

Under what conditions do you feel most compelled to attack?

When you attack, what do you do?

When you attack, how does it make you feel?

ACKNOWLEDGMENT COORDINATION

Complete each of the following sentences using the responses you have indicated above.

I am now aware that the way I attack is to

Which makes me feel

The next time I want to attack, I can choose to

In this way I will avoid

Now take a long, deep breath. You've just processed a lot of information, and YOU DONE GOOD! The list of descriptions provided is in no way exhaustive. It is just to get you started, to help you understand what you do, what you did, and what *you can choose not to do again*. It is important that you are able to identify your M.O. (modus operandi), because it holds very important clues that will help you make it through the *meantime*. No one is going to judge you, unless you judge yourself. Regardless of what you do or how you do it, if you really want to embrace your true Self, and find the love that is a part of that Self, you must be aware of what you do that is unloving. Once you become aware, you can make another choice.

Before you begin the next leg of the journey, take a few deep breaths. Make sure you are relaxed. You may want to think about a pleasant or calming situation. If nothing comes to mind, try reciting the following adaptation of the **Prayer of Protection:**

The light of God surrounds me.
The love of God enfolds me.
The power of God protects me.
The presence of God watches over me.
Wherever I am, God is.
Where there is God there is truth, peace, strength, and love.

STOP HERE!
YOU HAVE COMPLETED ONE EXERCISE.

love note
WHEREVER I AM . . .
GOD IS!

closing caring exercise

Read each of the following statements silently and then repeat
each of the statements aloud.

I declare W-A-R! I am now <u>W</u>illing, <u>A</u>ble, and <u>R</u>eady to eliminate
unconscious patterns that stand between me and love.

I am now *willing* to forgive. I am now *willing* to release. I am now
willing to be blessed.

I am now *able* to forgive. I am now *able* to release. I am now *able*
to be blessed.

I am now *ready* to forgive. I am now *ready* to release. I am now
ready to be blessed.

I am the Beloved. No thing and no one can change the truth of
my being.

For this I am so very grateful.

And So It Is!

FIRST FLOOR

this is the place! The most frustrating place of your life. It is a place where you know something is out of whack. Could it be you? It is also a place where even if you knew what was really going on, you would not have the strength, courage, or presence of mind to know what to do about it. In other words, you are in a place of tiredness, confusion, frustration and anxiety. And the last thing you want to do is work. Well, get a grip! You can't stop now! Take a deep breath and get to work.

On each of the worksheets that follow, you will be asked a series of questions designed to support you in healing and releasing nonproductive thoughts, feelings, perspectives, and behaviors. There is no right answer to any question. The key is to answer every question as honestly as you possibly can. This usually means responding with the first thought that comes to mind. Your first thought is most often your truest thought.

Be sure to complete the **Caring Exercise** before you begin any section. Once you have completed the worksheet, feel free to reread your responses and jot down any additional thoughts or feelings you may have. When you feel complete, meaning nothing else comes to mind, complete the **Closing Caring Exercise.** You may find it helpful to make a copy of a page before you begin, or use a notebook. In that way, you can repeat any exercise as often as you like to gain clarity and closure.

I wish you love!

caring exercise

Before beginning any section of the workbook, please care for yourself. Read each of the following statements silently and then repeat each of the statements aloud. Your words have power! Words create environment and experience. You are free to substitute for "God" any word that makes you comfortable.

I now allow myself to be in the presence of God's love.

I now give myself permission to feel the presence of God's love.

I now open my heart and mind to the healing power of God's love.

I now place my faith in the power and presence of God's love.

I now accept and affirm there is nothing I have done, can do, will do or experience that can separate me from God's love.

I now offer God's love to myself and extend it to everyone involved in my experience of life.

I am grateful that God's love is revealing itself to me.

IDENTIFY YOUR LOVE PATTERN

We are about to identify the energy in which you grew up. For that purpose we will call your responses to the following questions your *"love pattern."* Completing the following questions may help you gain clarity about why you do what you do in life and in relationships. Remember nothing, including you, can be wrong. So, make every attempt to answer the questions honestly without judgment, criticism, or censoring what you write down. When you complete this exercise, you will have the nuts and bolts, the ABC's of your love experience. Of course, even at your age, you can, if you choose to, relearn your ABC's!

Responses to the questions in this section need not be limited to parents. The process works for all caretakers (e.g. grandmother, grandfather, aunt, uncle, foster mother or father, adoptive mother or father, etc.). You can also complete this section whether the person in question is living or not. If you had more than one caretaker, you may use this exercise for each one.

LOVE PATTERN SURVEY

A. What my mother taught me about love is

B. She taught me this by the way she always

C. Translate your response to the preceding question into three words. My mother taught that love is

D. Use the preceding three words to complete this sentence:
    I **feel** love is

E. What my father taught me about love is

F. He taught me this by the way he always

G. Translate your response to the preceding question into three words. My father taught me that love is

H. Use the preceding three words to complete this sentence:
    I **think** love is

I. My first real love experience was

J. As a result of this experience, I learned

K. Translate your response to the preceding question into three words. My own experience has taught me that love is

L. Use the preceding three words to complete this sentence:
    I **know** love is

M. As a child, the love I saw at home / around me was

N. This made me feel

O. Translate your response to the preceding question into three words. The love I saw when growing up taught me that love is

P. Use the preceding three words to complete this sentence:
    I **believe** love is

Looking back at your responses to the previous questions, complete each of the following statements

Q. I *feel* love is

R. I *think* love is

S. I *know* love is

T. I *believe* love is

U. Bringing your awareness to a recent or present relationship, complete the following sentence:
The relationship I am having/have had with _____ is

V. This relationship makes/made me feel

W. Translate this relationship experience into three words.

Compare these three words to your responses for Items D, G, and K. How do these words support or conflict with what you feel, think, know, believe about love. *(Revisit your responses to Items Q, R, S, and T.)*

X. My response supports what I feel/think/know/believe about love because

Y. My response conflicts with what I feel/think/know/believe about love because

Z. I am now aware that I have experienced love in a way that makes me feel

I now choose to experience love in my life in a way that makes me feel

WRITE THE FOLLOWING SENTENCES
NINE TIMES

(Use your nondominant hand. If you are right-handed use your left, left-handed use your right.)

I now forgive myself for believing I have ever done anything wrong.

I now forgive myself for believing anyone has ever done anything wrong.

STOP HERE!

YOU HAVE COMPLETED ONE EXERCISE.

love note

EVEN WHEN MY FATHER AND MY MOTHER CAST
ME OFF, THE LOVE, THE LIGHT, THE POWER OF
GOD CAN AND WILL LIFT ME UP!

closing caring exercise

Read each of the following statements silently and then repeat
each of the statements aloud.

I declare W-A-R! I am now Willing, Able, and Ready to eliminate
unconscious patterns that stand between me and love.

I am now *willing* to forgive. I am now *willing* to release. I am now
willing to be blessed.

I am now *able* to forgive. I am now *able* to release. I am now *able*
to be blessed.

I am now *ready* to forgive. I am now *ready* to release. I am now
ready to be blessed.

I am the Beloved. No thing and no one can change the truth of
my being.

For this I am so very grateful.

And So It Is!

clearing emotional triggers

The feminine, the mother, represents the heart. Your earliest experiences with feminine energy create the essence of what you feel. This section can be used for any maternal caretakers (e.g. grandmother, aunt, foster mother, adoptive mother, etc.). It can be used whether the person in question is living or not. If you had more than one maternal caretaker, you may use this exercise for each one. *Before beginning,* **go to the Caring Exercise.**

A. At its best, my relationship with my mother is/was

B. I think of/remember my mother as being *(use positive trigger words)*

C. This makes/made me feel

D. The best thing I remember about our relationship is

E. This makes/made me feel

F. The most loving thing my mother said/did was

G. This makes/made me feel

H. At its worst, my relationship with my mother is/was

I. I think of/remember my mother as being *(use negative trigger words)*

J. This makes/made me feel

K. The worst thing I remember about our relationship is

L. This makes/made me feel

M. The most unloving thing my mother ever said/did was

N. This makes/made me feel

O. The one thing I wish my mother would do/had done for me is

P. The one thing I wish my mother would not do/had not done for me is

Q. The thing I wish I could do/could have done for my mother is

R. What I wish to say to my mother about our relationship is

S. The person in my life today who reminds me of my mother is

T. I think of this person as being *(use positive and negative triggers if necessary)*

U. This makes me feel

V. My relationship with this person is

W. This makes me feel

X. The most loving thing this person does / has done for me is

Y. This relationship reminds me of my relationship with my mother because *(revisit your response to A)*

Z. This relationship is different from my relationship with my mother because

AWARENESS COORDINATION

A. I am now aware that my relationship with my mother teaches me / taught me that love makes you feel *(rewrite your responses to C, E, and G)*

B. What I am learning/have learned and am willing to heal is the belief that love also makes you feel *(rewrite your responses to J, L, and N)*

C. To facilitate this healing, I am willing to

D. I am choosing to experience love in a way that makes me feel

WRITE THE FOLLOWING SENTENCES
NINE TIMES

(Use your nondominant hand. If you are right-handed use your left, left-handed use your right.)

I now forgive myself for believing my mother has ever done anything wrong.

I now forgive myself for believing anyone has ever done anything wrong.

STOP HERE!
YOU HAVE COMPLETED ONE EXERCISE.

love note
THE PAST IS THE FUTURE CONCEALED.
THE PRESENT IS THE PAST REVEALED.

closing caring exercise

Read each of the following statements silently and then repeat each of the statements aloud.

I declare W-A-R! I am now <u>W</u>illing, <u>A</u>ble, and <u>R</u>eady to eliminate unconscious patterns that stand between me and love.

I am now *willing* to forgive. I am now *willing* to release. I am now *willing* to be blessed.

I am now *able* to forgive. I am now *able* to release. I am now *able* to be blessed.

I am now *ready* to forgive. I am now *ready* to release. I am now *ready* to be blessed.

I am the Beloved. No thing and no one can change the truth of my being.

For this I am so very grateful.

And So It Is!

clearing mental triggers

The masculine, the father, represents the mind. Your earliest experiences with masculine energy create the essence of what you think. This section can be used for any paternal caretakers (e.g. grandfather, uncle, foster father, adoptive father, etc.). It can be used whether the person in question is living or not. If you had more than one paternal caretaker, you may use this exercise for each one. First, **go to the Caring Exercise.**

A. At its best, my relationship with my father is/was

B. I think of/remember my father as being *(use positive or negative triggers if necessary)*

C. This makes/made me feel

D. The best thing I remember about our relationship is

E. This makes/made me feel

F. The most loving thing my father said/did

G. This makes/made me feel

H. At its worst, my relationship with my father is/was

I. I think of / remember my father as being

J. This makes / made me feel

K. The worst thing I remember about our relationship is

L. This makes / made me feel

M. The most unloving thing my father ever said / did was

N. This makes/made me feel

O. The one thing I wish my father would do/had done for me is

P. The one thing I wish my father would not do/had not done for me is

Q. The thing I wish I could do/could have done for my father is

R. What I wish to say to my father about our relationship is

S. The person in my life today who reminds me of my father is

T. I think of this person as being *(use positive and negative triggers if necessary)*

U. This makes me feel

V. My relationship with this person is

W. This makes me feel

X. The most loving thing this person does/has done for me is

Y. This relationship reminds me of my relationship with my father because *(revisit your response to A)*

Z. This relationship is different from my relationship with my father because

AWARENESS COORDINATION

A. I am now aware that my relationship with my father teaches me/taught me that love makes you feel *(rewrite your responses to C, E, and G)*

B. What I am learning/have learned and am willing to heal is the belief that love also makes you feel *(rewrite your responses to J, L, and N)*

C. To facilitate this healing, I am willing to

D. I am choosing to experience love in a way that makes me feel

WRITE THE FOLLOWING SENTENCES
NINE TIMES.

(Use your nondominant hand. If you are right-handed use your left, left-handed use your right.)

I now forgive myself for believing my father has ever done anything wrong.

I now forgive myself for believing anyone has ever done anything wrong.

STOP HERE!
YOU HAVE COMPLETED ONE EXERCISE.

love note
DO NOT BE FOOLED BY APPEARANCES!
YOU CAN ALWAYS RELY ON THE DIVINE LOVE OF GOD.

closing caring exercise

Read each of the following statements silently and then repeat each of the statements aloud.

I declare W-A-R! I am now <u>W</u>illing, <u>A</u>ble, and <u>R</u>eady to eliminate unconscious patterns that stand between me and love.

I am now *willing* to forgive. I am now *willing* to release. I am now *willing* to be blessed.

I am now *able* to forgive. I am now *able* to release. I am now *able* to be blessed.

I am now *ready* to forgive. I am now *ready* to release. I am now *ready* to be blessed.

I am the Beloved. No thing and no one can change the truth of my being.

For this I am so very grateful.

And So It Is!

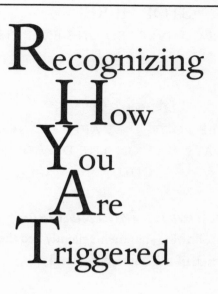

Recognizing

How

You

Are

Triggered

Will avoid a riot!

caring exercise

Before beginning any section of the workbook, please care for yourself. Read each of the following statements silently and then repeat each of the statements aloud. Your words have power! Words create environment and experience. You are free to substitute for *"God"* any word that makes you comfortable.

I now allow myself to be in the presence of God's love.

I now give myself permission to feel the presence of God's love.

I now open my heart and mind to the healing power of God's love.

I now place my faith in the power and presence of God's love.

I now accept and affirm there is nothing I have done, can do, will do or experience that can separate me from God's love.

I now offer God's love to myself and extend it to everyone involved in my experience of life.

I am grateful that God's love is revealing itself to me.

ACKNOWLEDGMENT COORDINATION

Now that you are aware of your love patterns, fear-based behaviors, and unconscious responses, let us see how it all fits together in the context of your relationships. As used throughout this book, a relationship refers to your interaction with people, and not just those with whom you are romantically involved. Feel free to use these pages to examine any relationship in which you are not having the experience you desire (e.g. at work, with friends, with children, etc.). Of course, the relationships that have the greatest impact on you are your loving relationships.

A. I am now willing to explore the experience of my relationship with

B. At its best this relationship is/was

C. This makes/made me feel *(use trigger words if necessary)*

D. This relationship resembles/resembled my relationship with (identify a caretaker if applicable)

Because

E. At its worst, the relationship is/was

F. This makes/made me feel

G. When I feel/felt this way, what I do/did is *(revisit your responses on pages 34–49 and 55–68)*

H. I respond/responded this way because
I felt

I thought

I believed

I knew

I. What I expected/asked for in this relationship was

J. When I realized I was not receiving what I asked for, what I did was

K. This makes/made me feel

L. When I feel/felt this way, what I do/did was

M. As a result, what is happening/what happened in the relationship was

N. When this happens/happened, I feel/felt angry because

O. When this happened, I feel/felt afraid because

P. I now realize what I do/did that was unloving is/was

Q. Responding this way made me feel

R. I am now aware that when I experience anger, I can choose to

S. I acknowledge that what I am learning/have learned and am willing to heal is the belief that love also makes you feel *(rewrite your responses to F, G, K, and Q)*

T. To facilitate this healing, I am willing to

U. I am now choosing to experience love in a way that makes me feel *(use trigger words if necessary)*

WRITE THE FOLLOWING SENTENCES
NINE TIMES.

(Use your nondominant hand. If you are right-handed use your left, left-handed use your right.)

I now forgive myself for believing I have ever done anything wrong.

I now forgive myself for believing anyone has ever done anything wrong.

STOP HERE!
YOU HAVE COMPLETED ONE EXERCISE

love note

TO BE WILLING TO DISPEL OLD HABITS THAT MAY BE INGRAINED INTO THE MIND IS TO BE WILLING TO REACT DIFFERENTLY TO CIRCUMSTANCES AND CONDITIONS. AND TO HAVE CIRCUMSTANCES AND CONDITIONS REACT DIFFERENTLY TO YOU!

closing caring exercise

Read each of the following statements silently and then repeat each of the statements aloud.

I declare W-A-R! I am now <u>W</u>illing, <u>A</u>ble, and <u>R</u>eady to eliminate unconscious patterns that stand between me and love.

I am now *willing* to forgive. I am now *willing* to release. I am now *willing* to be blessed.

I am now *able* to forgive. I am now *able* to release. I am now *able* to be blessed.

I am now *ready* to forgive. I am now *ready* to release. I am now *ready* to be blessed.

I am the Beloved. No thing and no one can change the truth of my being.

For this I am so very grateful.

And So It Is!

SECOND FLOOR

by the time you have made it this far, you probably have a pretty good idea about why you are where you are. Hopefully, you also have a better idea about where you want to go. The purpose of the second floor is to get clear about what has been holding you back or contributing to your slow movement.

On each of the worksheets that follow, you will be asked a series of questions designed to support you in recognizing the memories and experiences that may be holding you back. There is no "right" answer to any question. The key is to answer every question as honestly as you possibly can. This usually means responding with the first thought that comes to mind. Your first thought is most often your truest thought.

Be sure to complete the **Caring Exercise** before you begin any worksheet. Once you have completed the worksheet, feel free to reread your responses and jot down any additional thoughts or feelings you may have. When you feel complete, meaning nothing else comes to mind, complete the **Closing Caring Exercise.** You may find it helpful to make a copy of a page before you begin, or use a notebook. In that way, you can repeat any exercise as often as you like to gain clarity and closure.

I wish you love!

caring exercise

Before beginning any section of the workbook, please care for yourself. Read each of the following statements silently and then repeat each of the statements aloud. Your words have power! Words create environment and experience. You are free to substitute for "God" any word that makes you comfortable.

I now allow myself to be in the presence of God's love.

I now give myself permission to feel the presence of God's love.

I now open my heart and mind to the healing power of God's love.

I now place my faith in the power and presence of God's love.

I now accept and affirm there is nothing I have done, can do, will do or experience that can separate me from God's love.

I now offer God's love to myself and extend it to everyone involved in my experience of life.

I am grateful that God's love is revealing itself to me.

cleaning out disappointment

Turn to the Glossary to get a working definition of this experience. Complete the **Caring Exercise** before you begin this worksheet.

A. I am experiencing disappointment as it relates to *(identify one experience at a time)*

B. I believe my experience right now would be different if

C. My desired experience did not / has not happened because

D. What I expected to happen was

E. What I asked for was

F. When I did not get what I expected or asked for, what I did was

G. I responded in this way because I felt/believed

H. I now realize that when *(review your response from F)*

I experience disappointment.

WRITE THE FOLLOWING SENTENCES
NINE TIMES

(Use your nondominant hand. If you are right-handed use your left, left-handed use your right.)

I now forgive myself for believing I have ever done anything wrong.

I now forgive myself for believing anyone has ever done anything wrong.

ACKNOWLEDGMENT COORDINATION

A. I am now aware that the way I contribute to being disappointed is *(use your response from H)*

B. Which makes me feel

C. I now realize that I can choose to

D. Responding this way would make me feel

THE WAY TO ELIMINATE BEING DISAPPOINTED IS:

1. Ask for exactly what you what.
2. Clearly identify and communicate your expectations to yourself and to others involved in the experience.
3. Do not expect people to do for you what you can do for yourself.
4. Surrender all outcomes by being open to all experiences without judgment or criticism.
5. Accept responsibility for everything you do and experience.
6. Choose to see the lesson rather than disappointment.

STOP HERE!
YOU HAVE COMPLETED ONE EXERCISE

love note
POINTING THE FINGER IS THE WAY YOU DENY
THAT YOU HAVE HAD ANY INVOLVEMENT IN
CREATING THE EXPERIENCE. IT IS THE WAY YOU
DENY YOUR POWER.

closing caring exercise
Read each of the following statements silently and then repeat
each of the statements aloud.

I declare W-A-R! I am now <u>W</u>illing, <u>A</u>ble, and <u>R</u>eady to eliminate
unconscious patterns that stand between me and love.

I am now *willing* to forgive. I am now *willing* to release. I am now
willing to be blessed.

I am now *able* to forgive. I am now *able* to release. I am now *able*
to be blessed.

I am now *ready* to forgive. I am now *ready* to release. I am now
ready to be blessed.

I am the Beloved. No thing and no one can change the truth of
my being.

For this I am so very grateful.

And So It Is!

clearing up disappointment

Turn to the Glossary to get a working definition of this experience. Complete the **Caring Exercise** before you begin this worksheet.

Bringing to mind a recent experience in which you felt disappointed, respond to the following questions:

A. I am experiencing disappointment about

B. What I expected from this *(circle the appropriate response)*
   Job   Person   Relationship   Situation   was

C. I communicated this when I said

D. I know I was heard because

E. When I realized my expectations were not being met, I felt

F. I did / did not communicate how I was feeling because
I thought

I felt

I believed

I knew

G. I now understand that the most loving way I could have responded would have been to

H. This would have made me feel

I. This experience has taught me

WRITE THE FOLLOWING SENTENCES
NINE TIMES

(Use your nondominant hand. If you are right-handed use your left, left-handed use your right.)

I now forgive myself for believing I have ever done anything wrong.

I now forgive myself for believing that anyone has ever done anything wrong.

STOP HERE!
YOU HAVE COMPLETED ONE EXERCISE.

love note
NEVER UNDERESTIMATE THE ABILITY OF THE HUMAN MIND TO FORGET OR TO CHANGE!

closing caring exercise

Read each of the following statements silently and then repeat each of the statements aloud.

I declare W-A-R! I am now <u>W</u>illing, <u>A</u>ble, and <u>R</u>eady to eliminate unconscious patterns that stand between me and love.

I am now *willing* to forgive. I am now *willing* to release. I am now *willing* to be blessed.

I am now *able* to forgive. I am now *able* to release. I am now *able* to be blessed.

I am now *ready* to forgive. I am now *ready* to release. I am now *ready* to be blessed.

I am the Beloved. No thing and no one can change the truth of my being.

For this I am so very grateful.

And So It Is!

cleaning out betrayal

Turn to the Glossary to get a working definition of this experience. Complete the **Caring Exercise** before you begin this worksheet.

A. My earliest experience of feeling betrayed was when

B. I believe that as a result of that experience I

C. I believe this experience was the result of/ caused by

D. The most difficult part for me to accept/understand is

E. I did/did not communicate how I was feeling because
I thought

I felt

I believed

I knew

F. I now understand that the most loving way I could have responded would have been to

G. This would have made me feel

H. This experience has taught me

WRITE THE FOLLOWING SENTENCES
NINE TIMES

(Use your nondominant hand. If you are right-handed use your left, left-handed use your right.)

I now forgive myself for believing I have ever done anything wrong.

I now forgive myself for believing that anyone has ever done anything wrong.

STOP HERE!
YOU HAVE COMPLETED ONE EXERCISE.

love note
PEOPLE DO WHAT THEY DO BASED ON WHO
THEY ARE AND THE INFORMATION THEY HAVE
AT THE TIME. IF THEY KNEW BETTER, THEY
WOULD DO BETTER.

closing caring exercise
Read each of the following statements silently and then repeat
each of the statements aloud.

I declare W-A-R! I am now <u>W</u>illing, <u>A</u>ble, and <u>R</u>eady to eliminate
unconscious patterns that stand between me and love.

I am now *willing* to forgive. I am now *willing* to release. I am now
willing to be blessed.

I am now *able* to forgive. I am now *able* to release. I am now *able*
to be blessed.

I am now *ready* to forgive. I am now *ready* to release. I am now
ready to be blessed.

I am the Beloved. No thing and no one can change the truth of
my being.

For this I am so very grateful.

And So It Is!

clearing up betrayal

Turn to the Glossary to get a working definition of this experience. Complete the **Caring Exercise** before you begin this worksheet.

A. I am feeling betrayed by *(identify one person or experience at a time)*

B. I feel this way because

C. I had a similar experience when

D. In both experiences, what I expected to happen was

E. What I asked for was

F. When I realized that what I expected and asked for was not forthcoming, what I did was

G. It is / was difficult for me to accept

H. What I did when I could not accept what I felt / saw was

I. This made me feel

J. I now realize that when I *(use your responses from H)*

I experience betrayal.

WRITE THE FOLLOWING SENTENCES
NINE TIMES

(Use your nondominant hand. If you are right-handed use your left, left-handed use your right.)

I now forgive myself for believing I have ever done anything wrong.

I now forgive myself for believing that anyone has ever done anything wrong.

STOP HERE!
YOU HAVE COMPLETED ONE EXERCISE.

love note
RESPECT YOURSELF AND OTHER PEOPLE
ENOUGH TO TELL THEM THE TRUTH ABOUT
WHAT YOU FEEL WHEN YOU FEEL IT. DIALOGUE
GIVES BIRTH TO MIRACULOUS CHANGES!

closing caring exercise

Read each of the following statements silently and then repeat
each of the statements aloud.

I declare W-A-R! I am now <u>W</u>illing, <u>A</u>ble, and <u>R</u>eady to eliminate
unconscious patterns that stand between me and love.

I am now *willing* to forgive. I am now *willing* to release. I am now
willing to be blessed.

I am now *able* to forgive. I am now *able* to release. I am now *able*
to be blessed.

I am now *ready* to forgive. I am now *ready* to release. I am now
ready to be blessed.

I am the Beloved. No thing and no one can change the truth of
my being.

For this I am so very grateful.

And So It Is!

clearing up betrayal 2

Turn to the Glossary to get a working definition of this experience. Complete the **Caring Exercise** before you begin this worksheet.

1. On the top row of the chart on the next page, identify a recent experience (within the last ten years) and the people by whom you feel/have felt betrayed.

2. In the boxes below each name, identify your behavior (what you did/did not do) in your experience in the situation with the person whose name appears at the top of the column. *(If you do not know, check the Loving Behavior Reference on page 18.)*

3. Complete the entire column before moving on to the next.

i felt betrayed by/when

4. When you have completed the chart, reread each column and identify the behaviors common to each experience. List the recurring behaviors here, placing the one that occurred most often first, and the others in descending order.

1.

2.

3.

4.

5.

6.

7.

8.

9.

The above represent the unconscious behavior patterns that may contribute to the experience of betrayal. Rather than these behaviors, in a similar experience I can choose to

WRITE THE FOLLOWING SENTENCES
NINE TIMES

(Use your nondominant hand. If you are right-handed use your left, left-handed use your right.)

I now forgive myself for believing I have ever done anything wrong.

I now forgive myself for believing that anyone has ever done anything wrong.

STOP HERE!
YOU HAVE COMPLETED ONE EXERCISE.

love note
SELF-HEALING IS THE GIFT YOU OFFER TO THE WORLD. ALL THAT YOU ACCEPT FOR, DO FOR, AND OFFER TO YOURSELF, YOU PASS ON TO ALL WITH WHOM YOU COME INTO CONTACT.

closing caring exercise
Read each of the following statements silently and then repeat each of the statements aloud.

I declare W-A-R! I am now <u>W</u>illing, <u>A</u>ble, and <u>R</u>eady to eliminate unconscious patterns that stand between me and love.

I am now *willing* to forgive. I am now *willing* to release. I am now *willing* to be blessed.

I am now *able* to forgive. I am now *able* to release. I am now *able* to be blessed.

I am now *ready* to forgive. I am now *ready* to release. I am now *ready* to be blessed.

I am the Beloved. No thing and no one can change the truth of my being.

For this I am so very grateful.

And So It Is!

BETWEEN THE SECOND AND THIRD FLOORS

this is the place you come to get clear about your "stuff." A *meantime* experience at this level has nothing to do with what anyone has done to you or not done for you. This is all about you! This is about why you do what you do the way you do it. This is about self-reflection and self-acceptance. This is about moving out of shame, guilt, fear, anger, suffering, struggling, and drama into your true identity as the Beloved.

A *meantime* experience here is not about what you have been through. It is about how you went through it, what you gained, and how much love you demonstrate when your back is to the wall. Your hard times tell a lot about you. When you are in the *meantime,* if you are not willing or ready to examine yourself and your stuff, chances are you will end up back down in the basement.

Be sure to complete the **Caring Exercise** before you begin any worksheet. Once you have completed the worksheet, feel free to reread your answers and jot down any additional thoughts or feelings you may have. When you feel complete, meaning nothing else comes to mind, do the **Closing Caring Exercise.** You may find it helpful to make a copy of a page before you begin, or use a notebook; in that way, you can repeat an exercise as often as you like to gain clarity and closure.

I wish you love!

caring exercise

Before beginning any section of the workbook, please care for yourself. Read each of the following statements silently and then repeat each of the statements aloud. Your words have power! Words create environment and experience. You are free to substitute for "God" any word that makes you comfortable.

I now allow myself to be in the presence of God's love.

I now give myself permission to feel the presence of God's love.

I now open my heart and mind to the healing power of God's love.

I now place my faith in the power and presence of God's love.

I now accept and affirm there is nothing I have done, can do, will do or experience that can separate me from God's love.

I now offer God's love to myself and extend it to everyone involved in my experience of life.

I am grateful that God's love is revealing itself to me.

cleaning out shame

Turn to the Glossary to get a definition of this experience. Complete the **Caring Exercise** before you begin this worksheet.

A. The experience in my past I feel most ashamed of is

B. As a result of this experience I believe

C. As a result of this experience I have/have not

D. This experience made me feel

E. What I did that was not loving was

F. What I failed to do was

G. In a similar situation today, I would be willing to

H. Today, I am willing to release all thoughts, feelings, beliefs, behaviors, and motivations that create shame as it relates to *(rewrite your response to A)*

I. By releasing this experience I am choosing to experience

WRITE THE FOLLOWING SENTENCES
NINE TIMES

(Use your nondominant hand. If you are right-handed use your left, left-handed use your right.)

I now forgive myself for believing I have ever done anything wrong.

I now forgive myself for believing anyone has ever done anything wrong.

STOP HERE!
YOU HAVE COMPLETED ONE EXERCISE.

love note

SPIRITUAL HEALING REQUIRES A WILLINGNESS
TO FORGIVE, THE COURAGE TO RELEASE FEAR,
AND READINESS TO RELINQUISH ANGER,
HATRED, GUILT, AND SHAME. IT IS IN THESE
ACTS WE DEVELOP THE ABILITY TO SEE GOD IN
EVERYONE, INCLUDING OURSELVES.

closing caring exercise

Read each of the following statements silently and then repeat
each of the statements aloud.

I declare W-A-R! I am now <u>W</u>illing, <u>A</u>ble, and <u>R</u>eady to eliminate
unconscious patterns that stand between me and love.

I am now *willing* to forgive. I am now *willing* to release. I am now
willing to be blessed.

I am now *able* to forgive. I am now *able* to release. I am now *able*
to be blessed.

I am now *ready* to forgive. I am now *ready* to release. I am now
ready to be blessed.

I am the Beloved. No thing and no one can change the truth of
my being.

For this I am so very grateful.

And So It Is!

clearing up shame

Complete the **Caring Exercise** before you begin this worksheet.

A. I feel most ashamed of myself / my life / my past when

B. What this feels like is

C. When I have this feeling I am prone to *(revisit your responses on pages 35–38)*

D. What I need most at the time I feel ashamed is

E. If I had this I believe I would feel

F. What I can *do for myself* when I feel this way is

G. The next time I experience shame I can choose to

H. The next time I feel ashamed what I must remember is

I. I now declare W-A-R on all thoughts, feelings, memories, behaviors, intentions, and motivations that create shame, because I know *(rewrite your responses to G and H)*

WRITE THE FOLLOWING SENTENCES
NINE TIMES

(Use your nondominant hand. If you are right-handed use your left, left-handed use your right.)

I now forgive myself for believing I have ever done anything wrong.

I now forgive myself for believing anyone has ever done anything wrong.

STOP HERE!
YOU HAVE COMPLETED ONE EXERCISE.

love note
GOD IS AS DEPENDENT ON YOU AS YOU ARE ON GOD!

closing caring exercise

Read each of the following statements silently and then repeat each of the statements aloud.

I declare W-A-R! I am now Willing, Able, and Ready to eliminate unconscious patterns that stand between me and love.

I am now *willing* to forgive. I am now *willing* to release. I am now *willing* to be blessed.

I am now *able* to forgive. I am now *able* to release. I am now *able* to be blessed.

I am now *ready* to forgive. I am now *ready* to release. I am now *ready* to be blessed.

I am the Beloved. No thing and no one can change the truth of my being.

For this I am so very grateful.

And So It Is!

cleaning out guilt

Turn to the Glossary to get a definition of this experience. Complete the **Caring Exercise** before you begin this worksheet.

A. The experience in my past I feel most guilty about is

B. As a result of this experience I believe

C. As a result of this experience I have / have not

D. This experience made me feel

E. What I did that was not loving was

F. What I failed to do was

G. In a similar situation today, I would be willing to

H. Today, I am willing to release all thoughts, feelings, beliefs, behaviors, and motivations of guilt that relate to *(rewrite your response to A)*

I. By releasing this experience I am choosing to experience

WRITE THE FOLLOWING SENTENCES
NINE TIMES

(Use your nondominant hand. If you are right-handed use your left, left-handed use your right.)

I now forgive myself for believing I have ever done anything wrong.

I now forgive myself for believing that anyone has ever done anything wrong.

STOP HERE!
YOU HAVE COMPLETED ONE EXERCISE.

love note

ONLY THE TRUTH CAN SET YOU FREE, BRING ABOUT TOTAL HEALING, A LASTING RESOLUTION, AND THE ABILITY TO AVOID RE-CREATION OF A SIMILAR PROBLEM IN THE FUTURE.

closing caring exercise

Read each of the following statements silently and then repeat each of the statements aloud.

I declare W-A-R! I am now <u>W</u>illing, <u>A</u>ble, and <u>R</u>eady to eliminate unconscious patterns that stand between me and love.

I am now *willing* to forgive. I am now *willing* to release. I am now *willing* to be blessed.

I am now *able* to forgive. I am now *able* to release. I am now *able* to be blessed.

I am now *ready* to forgive. I am now *ready* to release. I am now *ready* to be blessed.

I am the Beloved. No thing and no one can change the truth of my being.

For this I am so very grateful.

And So It Is!

133

clearing up guilt

Complete the **Caring Exercise** before you begin this worksheet.

A. I feel most guilty about myself / my life / my past when

B. What this feels like is

C. When I have this feeling I am prone to *(revisit your responses on page 35–38)*

D. What I need most at the time I feel guilty is

E. If I had this I believe I would feel

F. What I can *do for myself* when I feel guilty is

G. The next time I experience guilt I can choose to

H. The next time I feel guilty what I must remember is

I. I now declare W-A-R on all thoughts, feelings, memories, behaviors, intentions, and motivations that create guilt because I know *(rewrite your responses to G and H)*

WRITE THE FOLLOWING SENTENCES
NINE TIMES

(Use your nondominant hand. If you are right-handed use your left, left-handed use your right.)

I now forgive myself for believing I have ever done anything wrong.

I now forgive myself for believing that anyone has ever done anything wrong.

STOP HERE!
YOU HAVE COMPLETED ONE EXERCISE.

love note

LINKING THE FUTURE TO THE PAIN OF THE PAST
DOES NOT ALLOW THE LIGHT OF PEACE, LOVE,
OR JOY TO COME IN.

closing caring exercise

Read each of the following statements silently and then repeat
each of the statements aloud.

I declare W-A-R! I am now <u>W</u>illing, <u>A</u>ble, and <u>R</u>eady to eliminate
unconscious patterns that stand between me and love.

I am now *willing* to forgive. I am now *willing* to release. I am now
willing to be blessed.

I am now *able* to forgive. I am now *able* to release. I am now *able*
to be blessed.

I am now *ready* to forgive. I am now *ready* to release. I am now
ready to be blessed.

I am the Beloved. No thing and no one can change the truth of
my being.

For this I am so very grateful.

And So It Is!

cleaning out anger

Turn to the Glossary to get a definition of this experience. Complete the **Caring Exercise** before you begin this worksheet.

A. The experience in my past I feel most angry about is

B. As a result of this experience I believe

C. As a result of this experience I have / have not

D. This experience made me feel

E. What I did that was not loving was

F. What I failed to do was

G. If I had another opportunity, I would be willing to

H. Today, I am willing to release all angry thoughts, feelings, beliefs, behaviors, and motivations that relate to *(rewrite your response to A)*

I. By releasing this experience I am choosing to experience

WRITE THE FOLLOWING SENTENCES
NINE TIMES

(Use your nondominant hand. If you are right-handed use your left, left-handed use your right.)

I now forgive myself for believing I have ever done anything wrong.

I now forgive myself for believing that anyone has ever done anything wrong.

STOP HERE!
YOU HAVE COMPLETED ONE EXERCISE.

love note

SPIRITUAL HEALING REQUIRES A WILLINGNESS TO FORGIVE, THE COURAGE TO RELEASE FEAR, AND READINESS TO RELINQUISH ANGER, HATRED, GUILT, AND SHAME. IT IS IN THESE ACTS WE DEVELOP THE ABILITY TO SEE GOD IN EVERYONE, INCLUDING OURSELVES.

closing caring exercise

Read each of the following statements silently and then repeat each of the statements aloud.

I declare W-A-R! I am now <u>W</u>illing, <u>A</u>ble, and <u>R</u>eady to eliminate unconscious patterns that stand between me and love.

I am now *willing* to forgive. I am now *willing* to release. I am now *willing* to be blessed.

I am now *able* to forgive. I am now *able* to release. I am now *able* to be blessed.

I am now *ready* to forgive. I am now *ready* to release. I am now *ready* to be blessed.

I am the Beloved. No thing and no one can change the truth of my being.

For this I am so very grateful.

And So It Is!

clearing up anger

Complete the **Caring Exercise** before you begin this worksheet.

A. When I think about myself/my life/my past, I get angry because

B. What this feels like is

C. When I feel angry I am prone to *(revisit your responses on pages 35–38)*

D. What I need most at the time I feel angry is

E. If I had this I believe I would feel

F. What I can *do for myself* when I feel angry is

G. The next time I experience anger I can choose to

H. The next time I feel angry what I must remember is

I. I now declare W-A-R on all thoughts, feelings, memories, behaviors, intentions, and motivations that contribute to anger because I know *(rewrite your responses to G and H)*

WRITE THE FOLLOWING SENTENCES
NINE TIMES

(Use your nondominant hand. If you are right-handed use your left, left-handed use your right.)

I now forgive myself for believing I have ever done anything wrong.

I now forgive myself for believing that anyone has ever done anything wrong.

STOP HERE!
YOU HAVE COMPLETED ONE EXERCISE.

love note
ANGRY? TRY A SMILE. IT CREATES FEWER
WRINKLES!

closing caring exercise

Read each of the following statements silently and then repeat
each of the statements aloud.

I declare W-A-R! I am now <u>W</u>illing, <u>A</u>ble, and <u>R</u>eady to eliminate
unconscious patterns that stand between me and love.

I am now *willing* to forgive. I am now *willing* to release. I am now
willing to be blessed.

I am now *able* to forgive. I am now *able* to release. I am now *able*
to be blessed.

I am now *ready* to forgive. I am now *ready* to release. I am now
ready to be blessed.

I am the Beloved. No thing and no one can change the truth of
my being.

For this I am so very grateful.

And So It Is!

cleaning out remorse

Turn to the Glossary to get a definition of this experience. Complete the **Caring Exercise** before you begin this worksheet.

A. The experience in my past I feel most remorseful about is

B. As a result of this experience I believe

C. As a result of this experience I have / have not

D. This experience made me feel

E. What I did that was not loving was

F. What I failed to do was

G. If I had another opportunity, I would be willing to

H. Today, I am willing to release all thoughts, feelings, beliefs, behaviors, and motivations that create remorse and that relate to *(rewrite your response to A)*

I. By releasing this experience I am choosing to experience

WRITE THE FOLLOWING SENTENCES
NINE TIMES

(Use your nondominant hand. If you are right-handed use your left, left-handed use your right.)

I now forgive myself for believing I have ever done anything wrong.

I now forgive myself for believing that anyone has ever done anything wrong.

STOP HERE!
YOU HAVE COMPLETED ONE EXERCISE.

love note
IF YOU HOLD YOUR HAND OUT IN THE DARKNESS, GOD WILL TAKE YOUR HAND. IF YOU HOLD BOTH HANDS OUT IN THE DARKNESS, GOD AND GODDESS WILL LIFT YOU UP AND CARRY YOU TO EXACTLY WHERE YOU NEED TO GO.

closing caring exercise
Read each of the following statements silently and then repeat each of the statements aloud.

I declare W-A-R! I am now <u>W</u>illing, <u>A</u>ble, and <u>R</u>eady to eliminate unconscious patterns that stand between me and love.

I am now *willing* to forgive. I am now *willing* to release. I am now *willing* to be blessed.

I am now *able* to forgive. I am now *able* to release. I am now *able* to be blessed.

I am now *ready* to forgive. I am now *ready* to release. I am now *ready* to be blessed.

I am the Beloved. No thing and no one can change the truth of my being.

For this I am so very grateful.

And So It Is!

149

clearing up remorse

Complete the **Caring Exercise** before you begin this worksheet.

A. When I think about myself/my life/my past, I feel remorse because

B. What this feels like is

C. When I feel remorse I am prone to *(revisit your responses on pages 35–38)*

D. What I need most at the time I feel remorse is

E. If I had this I believe I would feel

F. What I can *do for myself* when I feel remorse is

G. The next time I experience remorse what I can choose to do is

H. The next time I feel remorse what I must remember is

I. I now declare W-A-R on all thoughts, feelings, memories, behaviors, intentions, and motivations that contribute to remorse because I know *(rewrite your responses to G and H)*

WRITE THE FOLLOWING SENTENCES
NINE TIMES

(Use your nondominant hand. If you are right-handed use your left, left-handed use your right.)

I now forgive myself for believing I have ever done anything wrong.

I now forgive myself for believing that anyone has ever done anything wrong.

STOP HERE!
YOU HAVE COMPLETED ONE EXERCISE.

love note
AS YOU RECOGNIZE THE POWER AND PRESENCE
OF GOD AS THE VERY ESSENCE OF YOUR BEING,
GOD'S LOVE SURROUNDS AND SUPPORTS YOU,
MOMENT BY MOMENT. YOU LIVE IN THE LIGHT
OF GOD'S LOVE ALWAYS.

closing caring exercise
Read each of the following statements silently and then repeat
each of the statements aloud.

I declare W-A-R! I am now <u>W</u>illing, <u>A</u>ble, and <u>R</u>eady to eliminate
unconscious patterns that stand between me and love.

I am now *willing* to forgive. I am now *willing* to release. I am now
willing to be blessed.

I am now *able* to forgive. I am now *able* to release. I am now *able*
to be blessed.

I am now *ready* to forgive. I am now *ready* to release. I am now
ready to be blessed.

I am the Beloved. No thing and no one can change the truth of
my being.

For this I am so very grateful.

And So It Is!

153

cleaning out fear

Turn to the Glossary to get a definition of this experience. Complete the **Caring Exercise** before you begin this worksheet.

A. My greatest fear is

B. If this happens I believe I would

C. If that happens I believe I would

D. My greatest fear is *(rewrite your response to C)*

E. When I experience this fear I feel

F. I am now aware that when I experience this fear I am prone to
(revisit your response to D)

G. What I can choose to do instead is

H. This would make me feel

I. If this happens I believe I would

J. If that happens I believe I would

K. I am now aware that the greatest fear in my life today is not experiencing *(rewrite your response to J)*

L. Today, I am willing to release all thoughts, feelings, beliefs, behaviors, and motivations that support fear as it relates to *(rewrite your response to A)*

WRITE THE FOLLOWING SENTENCES
NINE TIMES

(Use your nondominant hand. If you are right-handed use your left, left-handed use your right.)

I will fear no harm, no evil, no thing, no one.

The protecting and perfecting presence of good, of God, is available to me now. (Feel free to substitute for the word "God" any word with which you are comfortable.)

STOP HERE!
YOU HAVE COMPLETED ONE EXERCISE.

love note
IN A PLACE OF STILLNESS,
THERE IS A DROP OF PEACE.
IN A PLACE OF PEACE,
THERE IS A DROP OF LOVE.
IN A DROP OF LOVE,
THERE IS THE STILLNESS OF PEACE.
IN THE STILLNESS OF PEACE, THERE I AM!

closing caring exercise
Read each of the following statements silently and then repeat each of the statements aloud.

I declare W-A-R! I am now Willing, Able, and Ready to eliminate unconscious patterns that stand between me and love.

I am now *willing* to forgive. I am now *willing* to release. I am now *willing* to be blessed.

I am now *able* to forgive. I am now *able* to release. I am now *able* to be blessed.

I am now *ready* to forgive. I am now *ready* to release. I am now *ready* to be blessed.

I am the Beloved. No thing and no one can change the truth of my being.

For this I am so very grateful.

And So It Is!

clearing up fear

Procrastination is a form of fear. Here we will work through the issue of fear manifesting itself as procrastination—the art of putting things off. Complete the **Caring Exercise** before you begin this worksheet.

A. The best reasons I have to procrastinate are

B. When I do this it makes me feel

C. When I feel this way I am prone to (*revisit your responses on pages 35–38*)

D. When I respond this way it makes me feel

E. I am now aware that this is an unloving way to treat myself. It is a manifestation of the fear of

F. Rather than procrastinate, I can now choose to

G. Responding this way would give me a greater sense of

H. I now choose to experience a greater sense of *(rewrite your response from G)*

WRITE THE FOLLOWING SENTENCES
NINE TIMES

(Use your nondominant hand. If you are right-handed use your left, left-handed use your right.)

I now forgive myself for every unloving act ever committed against myself.

I now forgive myself totally and unconditionally.

STOP HERE!

YOU HAVE COMPLETED ONE EXERCISE.

love note

I CANNOT CHANGE MYSELF, HELP MYSELF, OR HEAL MYSELF. WHAT I *CAN* DO IS TRUST THE POWER AND PRESENCE OF DIVINE WILL TO REVEAL ITSELF IN ME, AS ME, AND THROUGH ME. THIS WILL CHANGE ME, HELP ME, AND HEAL ME.

closing caring exercise

Read each of the following statements silently and then repeat each of the statements aloud.

I declare W-A-R! I am now <u>W</u>illing, <u>A</u>ble, and <u>R</u>eady to eliminate unconscious patterns that stand between me and love.

I am now *willing* to forgive. I am now *willing* to release. I am now *willing* to be blessed.

I am now *able* to forgive. I am now *able* to release. I am now *able* to be blessed.

I am now *ready* to forgive. I am now *ready* to release. I am now *ready* to be blessed.

I am the Beloved. No thing and no one can change the truth of my being.

For this I am so very grateful.

And So It Is!

THIRD FLOOR

all relationships are healing opportunities. They provide us with the information we need to heal our minds and hearts. Those persons who agree to have a relationship with us, do so in love. They love us enough to spend some part of their lives in our healing process. All we ever need do in a relationship is to choose the experience we desire and assume full responsibility for creating that experience. While it may sound simple, those of us in the *meantime* of a relationship know that it is not. The key is to *identify the patterns of thought and behavior* that prohibit the realization of the experience and *make the necessary shift* to create a new experience.

This is the chapter where the *"shift"* happens! The third floor is the floor of creation. This is where we create love by learning to love! Creation of something new requires clarity about exactly what you desire. On each of the worksheets that follow, you will be asked a series of questions designed to help you ask for exactly what you want in life and in a loving, intimate relationship. There is no "right" answer to any question. The key is to answer every question as honestly as you possibly can. This usually means responding with the first thought that comes to mind. Your first thought is most often your truest thought.

Be sure to complete the **Caring Exercise** before you begin any worksheet. Once you have completed the worksheet, feel free to reread your responses and jot down any additional thoughts or feelings you may have. When you feel complete, meaning nothing else comes to mind, complete the **Closing Caring Exercise.** You may find it helpful to make a copy of a page before you begin or use a notebook; in that way, you can repeat any exercise as often as you like to gain clarity and closure.

I wish you love!

caring exercise

Before beginning any section of the workbook, please care for yourself. Read each of the following statements silently and then repeat each of the statements aloud. Your words have power! Words create environment and experience. You are free to substitute for "God" any word that makes you comfortable.

I now allow myself to be in the presence of God's love.

I now give myself permission to feel the presence of God's love.

I now open my heart and mind to the healing power of God's love.

I now place my faith in the power and presence of God's love.

I now accept and affirm there is nothing I have done, can do, will do or experience that can separate me from God's love.

I now offer God's love to myself and extend it to everyone involved in my experience of life.

I am grateful that God's love is revealing itself to me.

THE DIVINE ME

Respond to each of the following statements with the first thought that pops into your mind. Feel free to use the trigger words (see pages 26–27) whenever necessary.

1. I am the Beloved! The Beloved is

2. I know this because

3. I feel this because

4. I believe this because

5. I am the Beloved! The Beloved is

6. I know this because

7. I feel this because

8. I believe this because

9. I am the Beloved! The Beloved is

10. I know this because

11. I feel this because

12. I believe this because

13. I am the Beloved! The Beloved is

14. I know this because

15. I feel this because

16. I believe this because

17. I am the Beloved! I know, feel, and believe this because

18. The Beloved deserves to be

19. The Beloved deserves to have

20. The Beloved deserves to feel

21. The way the Beloved creates what the Beloved is, is by

22. The way the Beloved creates what the Beloved has is by

23. The way the Beloved creates what the Beloved feels is to

24. I am the Beloved! I create myself by

25. I am the Beloved! I create what I desire to experience by

26. I am the Beloved! I create what I feel by

STOP HERE!
YOU HAVE COMPLETED ONE EXERCISE.

love note
WHATEVER YOU FOCUS ON HAS A TREMENDOUS IMPACT ON *HOW* YOU LIVE AND *WHAT* YOU LIVE!

closing caring exercise
Read each of the following statements silently and then repeat each of the statements aloud.

I declare W-A-R! I am now <u>W</u>illing, <u>A</u>ble, and <u>R</u>eady to eliminate unconscious patterns that stand between me and love.

I am now *willing* to forgive. I am now *willing* to release. I am now *willing* to be blessed.

I am now *able* to forgive. I am now *able* to release. I am now *able* to be blessed.

I am now *ready* to forgive. I am now *ready* to release. I am now *ready* to be blessed.

I am the Beloved. No thing and no one can change the truth of my being.

For this I am so very grateful.

And So It Is!

MY DIVINE LIFE

Your divine mate is seeking you as diligently as you are seeking your divine mate! When s/he shows up, what is s/he going to find?

1. Using seven to nine adjectives, describe your life (e.g. family, social, professional, financial, health, etc.) as it is today

2. Using seven to nine adjectives describe how you *feel* about your life as it is today

3. Use a dictionary to define each of the words you have listed in Items 1 and 2.

a. My life is   DEFINITION

b. I feel my life is   DEFINITION

4. Review your responses in list 3a. Do you feel the definitions are

Accurate_____   Severe_____   Too Severe_____

5. Write below those definitions you believe are most accurate

6. If your divine mate were to show up today, what is the most loving explanation you could give of your life as described in 5?

7. Explain to your divine mate how his/her presence would make the experience of your life better.

8. As specifically as possible, identify exactly what you would ask your partner for in a relationship.

9. Review your responses in list 3b. Do you feel the definitions are
Accurate_____ Severe_____ Too Severe_____

10. Write below those responses you believe are most accurate.

11. If your divine mate were to show up today, what is the most loving explanation you could offer about the way you feel about your life as described in 10?

12. Explain to your divine mate how his/her presence would help you feel better about your life.

13. As specifically as possible, identify to your partner exactly how you want to feel in a relationship.

14. Review your responses to 7, 8, 12, and 13. Identify and describe how you can create these experiences for yourself.

STOP HERE!
YOU HAVE COMPLETED ONE EXERCISE.

love note

ONE OF THE GREATEST, MOST LOVING GIFTS
YOU CAN GIVE TO YOUR PARTNER IS YOUR
WHOLENESS.

closing caring exercise

Read each of the following statements silently and then repeat
each of the statements aloud.

I declare W-A-R! I am now <u>W</u>illing, <u>A</u>ble, and <u>R</u>eady to eliminate
unconscious patterns that stand between me and love.

I am now *willing* to forgive. I am now *willing* to release. I am now
willing to be blessed.

I am now *able* to forgive. I am now *able* to release. I am now *able*
to be blessed.

I am now *ready* to forgive. I am now *ready* to release. I am now
ready to be blessed.

I am the Beloved. No thing and no one can change the truth of
my being.

For this I am so very grateful.

And So It Is!

MY DIVINE MATE

You cannot have what you want until you know what it looks and feels like! In this section, you will begin to identify what you want and the experience you desire in a loving or intimate relationship. On each of the lines provided in the next section, use no more than five words per line to identify the *attributes, **not physical characteristics,*** you would like your divine mate to have. At the end of the section, complete the questions before you move on to the next section. The goal is to be as clear as possible about what you want, the experience you desire, and what it will feel like. It does not matter whether or not you are currently in a relationship, so don't try to match what you want with what you may or may not have. Go for the gusto!

The word "attribute" refers to a person's character, demeanor, frame of mind, what s/he likes to do, etc. For the purpose of this exercise, "attribute" does not refer to the way a person looks. The universe knows what you like and it specializes in precise delivery!

my divine mate

1. My divine mate is

2. My divine mate is

3. My divine mate is

4. My divine mate is

5. My divine mate is

6. My divine mate is

7. My divine mate is

8. My divine mate is

9. My divine mate is

GROUP A

To be in a relationship with a mate who possesses these qualities would make me feel

1.
2.
3.
4.
5.
6.
7.
8.
9.

GROUP B

B. To be in a relationship with a mate who does not possess these qualities would make me feel

1.
2.

3.

4.

5.

6.

7.

8.

9.

MY RELATIONSHIP WISH LIST

Now let's put it all together. Complete each of the statements below as directed.

1. My divine mate is *(choose **one word** from each line of the attributes you identified in "My Divine Mate," page 176)*

2. When I am in a relationship with a mate who possesses these qualities I feel *(choose and list one word from each line in Group A)*

3. To be in a relationship like this would remind me of *(identify a relationship or a memory that closely resembles your ideas of a divine relationship)*

4. When I am in a relationship with a mate **who does not** possess these qualities, I feel *(choose and list one word from each line in Group B)*

5. To be in a relationship like this would remind me of *(identify a relationship or a memory that does not match your ideals of a divine relationship)*

6. My current / most recent relationship does not / did not give me this experience because I felt

7. When I realized the relationship does not / did not fulfill my divine ideal, what I did was

8. I am now choosing to experience a relationship that allows me to feel *(list the experiences identified in 2)*

9. I now understand that I can have this experience when I *(identify what it is you believe you can do or stop doing that will allow you to create the experience of a divine relationship)*

10. I am now aware that the way I can create this experience in my life with or without a mate is to

STOP HERE!
YOU HAVE COMPLETED ONE EXERCISE.

love note

DYING TO WHO YOU ONCE WERE AND WHAT YOU ONCE KNEW IS THE PAIN OF THE LABOR REQUIRED TO BE WHO YOU WERE BORN TO BE. IT IS THE KIND OF PAIN REQUIRED TO LIVE!

closing caring exercise

Read each of the following statements silently and then repeat each of the statements aloud.

I declare W-A-R! I am now <u>W</u>illing, <u>A</u>ble, and <u>R</u>eady to eliminate unconscious patterns that stand between me and love.

I am now *willing* to forgive. I am now *willing* to release. I am now *willing* to be blessed.

I am now *able* to forgive. I am now *able* to release. I am now *able* to be blessed.

I am now *ready* to forgive. I am now *ready* to release. I am now *ready* to be blessed.

I am the Beloved. No thing and no one can change the truth of my being.

For this I am so very grateful.

And So It Is!

MY DIVINE EXPERIENCE

Respond to the following questions with the first thought that pops into your mind as it relates to relationships. Allow yourself to be completely honest with yourself.

1. What do you want?

2. What would you feel if this were your reality? *(use trigger words, if necessary)*

3. What is the experience (state of mind or being) you believe it will bring you?

4. What do you want?

5. What would you feel if this were your reality?

6. What is the experience (state of mind or being) you believe it will bring you?

7. What do you want?

8. What would you feel if this were your reality?

9. What is the experience (state of mind or being) you believe it will bring you?

10. What I want in my ideal relationship is *(rewrite your responses to 1, 4, and 7)*

11. My ideal relationship would feel *(rewrite your responses to 2, 5, and 8)*

12. In my ideal relationship I would experience *(rewrite your responses to 3, 6, and 9)*

13. I can create these experiences for myself by

STOP HERE!

YOU HAVE COMPLETED ONE EXERCISE.

love note

THINK OF EVERY NEGATIVE THING YOU HAVE
EVER THOUGHT OR SPOKEN ABOUT YOURSELF
AND ASK YOURSELF WHY YOU HAVEN'T BEEN
STRUCK DEAD! WHY? BECAUSE GOD FORGIVES
YOU! THAT'S WHY!

closing caring exercise

Read each of the following statements silently and then repeat
each of the statements aloud.

I declare W-A-R! I am now <u>W</u>illing, <u>A</u>ble, and <u>R</u>eady to eliminate
unconscious patterns that stand between me and love.

I am now *willing* to forgive. I am now *willing* to release. I am now
willing to be blessed.

I am now *able* to forgive. I am now *able* to release. I am now *able*
to be blessed.

I am now *ready* to forgive. I am now *ready* to release. I am now
ready to be blessed.

I am the Beloved. No thing and no one can change the truth of
my being.

For this I am so very grateful.

And So It Is!

184

MY IDEAL RELATIONSHIP

1. Describe how you wish to feel in a relationship.

2. What do you believe has prevented this from happening in past relationships?

3. Why do you believe it will / can happen now?

4. How will decisions be made in this relationship about this relationship?

5. How did you make decisions in past relationships?

6. How will resources (e.g. economic, social, etc.) be allocated in this relationship?

7. How were resources allocated in past relationships?

8. How will conflicts be resolved in this relationship?

9. How were conflicts resolved in past relationships?

10. What are you willing to do to support yourself in creating your ideal relationship?

11. How will you accomplish the things you have identified above?

STOP HERE!
YOU HAVE COMPLETED ONE EXERCISE.

love note
BEHOLD!
YOU ARE PREPARED TO DO A NEW THING!
BE BLESSED!

closing caring exercise

Read each of the following statements silently and then repeat each of the statements aloud.

I declare W-A-R! I am now <u>W</u>illing, <u>A</u>ble, and <u>R</u>eady to eliminate unconscious patterns that stand between me and love.

I am now *willing* to forgive. I am now *willing* to release. I am now *willing* to be blessed.

I am now *able* to forgive. I am now *able* to release. I am now *able* to be blessed.

I am now *ready* to forgive. I am now *ready* to release. I am now *ready* to be blessed.

I am the Beloved. No thing and no one can change the truth of my being.

For this I am so very grateful.

And So It Is!

THE ATTIC

congratulations! You have made it through all of the "stuff" that was holding you back! You have confronted the demons and slain the dragons! You have cleaned the house and are now ready to get on with your life! This means that you have found the love of your life! This means that you realize that you are the Beloved. Does this mean that the journey, the process, the healing is over? Now, I know you know better than that!!!

Your work in the attic is about never losing sight of who you are and your purpose for being on the planet. You are here to glorify and demonstrate your God self, your true Self. You are here to celebrate all that life offers. You are here to do what you love, and what brings you joy! You are now charged with the ability and duty to apply love, the essence of who you are, to everything you do. Your work from this point on is about being a light unto the world. This is the spiritual way, which is not always easy. But you know what? You are equipped—you beloved being, you!

caring exercise

Before beginning an exercise, read each of the following statements silently, and then repeat each of the statements aloud. Your
words have power! Words create environment and experience.
You are free to substitute for the word "God" any word that makes
you comfortable.

There is nothing to be healed only God to be revealed.
There is nothing to be healed only God to be revealed.
There is nothing to be healed only God to be revealed.
Thank you God for revealing yourself as peace in my life.
Thank you God for revealing yourself as joy in my life.
Thank you God for revealing yourself as the strength
of my life.
Thank you God for revealing yourself at the
center of my life.
Thank you God for defending me, protecting me, guiding me,
taking care of everything that concerns me, and doing
everything that is appointed to me.
Thank you God for healing my relationships,
protecting my children, healing my body, providing
for my every need.
Most of all God, thank you for loving me just as I am and
for knowing what I need and for being the fulfillment of
my needs, even before I ask.

Today, I acknowledge, I accept, I believe there is nothing that needs to be fixed, changed, or healed in me or about me, because God, my God, will always be revealed.
For this I am so very grateful.
And So It Is!

DAILY ACTS OF FAITH

ACTS is the acronym for *Acknowledgment, Confession, Thanksgiving, and Supplication.* It is a prayer process that can be used to develop a deeper relationship with God and your higher self. This process is to be used for nine consecutive days, each morning (immediately upon rising) and evening (just prior to retiring). Complete each response spontaneously, and complete an entire section before moving to the next. Feel free to substitute for the word "God" any word that makes you comfortable.

acknowledgment (Recognition of the Divine presence in your life and your deepest thoughts, feelings, ideas about that presence.)

1. Today, I acknowledge God as

2. Today, I acknowledge God as

3. Today, I acknowledge God as

4. Today, I acknowledge God as

5. Today, I acknowledge God as

6. Today, I acknowledge God as

7. Today, I acknowledge God as

8. Today, I acknowledge God as

9. Today, I acknowledge God as

confession (Acknowledgment of those things you have done that were unloving and not a reflection of your true Self.)

1. Today, I confess that I

and I forgive myself totally and unconditionally.

2. Today, I confess that I

and I forgive myself totally and unconditionally.

3. Today, I confess that I

and I forgive myself totally and unconditionally.

4. Today, I confess that I

and I forgive myself totally and unconditionally.

5. Today, I confess that I

and I forgive myself totally and unconditionally.

6. Today, I confess that I

and I forgive myself totally and unconditionally.

7. Today, I confess that I

and I forgive myself totally and unconditionally.

8. Today, I confess that I

and I forgive myself totally and unconditionally.

9. Today, I confess that I

and I forgive myself totally and unconditionally.

thanksgiving (Conscious acknowledgment and praise given in appreciation and gratitude for what you have received.)

1. Today, I thank God for

2. Today, I thank God for

3. Today, I thank God for

4. Today, I thank God for

5. Today, I thank God for

6. Today, I thank God for

7. Today, I thank God for

8. Today, I thank God for

9. Today, I thank God for

supplication (Requesting support, assistance, guidance, as it relates to a specific need / desire in your life.)

1. Today, I am asking for

and for this I am so grateful.

2. Today, I am asking for

and for this I am so grateful.

3. Today, I am asking for

and for this I am so grateful.

4. Today, I am asking for

and for this I am so grateful.

5. Today, I am asking for

and for this I am so grateful.

6. Today, I am asking for

and for this I am so grateful.

7. Today, I am asking for

and for this I am so grateful.

8. Today, I am asking for

and for this I am so grateful.

9. Today, I am asking for

and for this I am so grateful.

Once you have completed the entire exercise, spend a few moments in quiet contemplation.

STOP HERE!
YOU HAVE COMPLETED THE EXERCISE.

love note
WHEN YOU CAN BEGIN TO PRACTICE
SEEING AND REALIZING THE PRESENCE OF GOD
RIGHT IN THE MIDST OF WHAT IS GOING ON
OUT THERE, SOMETHING BEGINS TO HAPPEN
WITHIN YOU.

closing caring exercise

Read each of the following statements silently and then repeat each of the statements aloud. Let Us Pray!

Dear God:

This is the day that you have made, and I am so grateful to be a part of it.

This is the day that I have made up my mind to place myself totally in your care.

This is the day that all of my spiritual and karmic debts are canceled, and I am so grateful to be free.

On this day, I now declare and decree that I am free of fear! Free of doubt! Free of anger! Free of shame! Free of guilt! Free of unproductive thoughts and actions!

On this glorious day that you have allowed me to see I am divinely determined and dutifully dedicated to live the life that you have created for me.

A life of love, peace, joy, fulfillment, and creative activity.

This is the day, God!

Your day! My day!

And for this day, I am so very, very grateful.

And So It Is!

197

PRACTICING THE PRESENCE

1. What is your personal definition of spirituality?

2. In what ways do you practice spirituality according to this definition on a daily basis?

3. In what ways do you desire to experience more spirituality in your life?

4. What are you willing to do to create this experience?

5. What is your personal definition of love?

6. In what ways do you experience love on a daily basis?

7. In what ways do you desire to give more love?

8. What are you willing to offer to show love to people you are not fond of?

9. What is your personal definition of God?

10. In what ways do you experience God in your life on a daily basis?

11. In what ways do you desire to experience more of God in your life?

12. What are you willing to do to create this experience?

ACKNOWLEDGMENT COORDINATION

1. With regard to my spiritual life, I am now committed to creating a more spiritual experience by

2. With regard to my understanding of love, I am now committed to creating more love in my life by

3. With regard to my understanding of God, I am now committed to creating a greater experience of God by

4. In making the commitment to creating each of these experiences in my life, I am no longer willing to

STOP HERE!
YOU HAVE COMPLETED ALL THE EXERCISES.

love note

THROUGH THE CONSCIOUS RECOGNITION OF GOD IN EVERY SITUATION, WE NEVER MISS AN OPPORTUNITY TO BEHOLD THE BELOVED, THE PRECIOUS SPIRIT INHERENT IN EACH MOMENT WE ENCOUNTER WITH ANOTHER OF GOD'S CREATIONS.

closing caring exercise

Read each of the following statements silently and then repeat each of the statements aloud. Let Us Pray!

Dear God:

This is the day that you have made, and I am so grateful to be a part of it.

This is the day that I have made up my mind to place myself totally in your care.

This is the day that all of my spiritual and karmic debts are canceled, and I am so grateful to be free.

On this day, I now declare and decree that I am free of fear! Free of doubt! Free of anger! Free of shame! Free of guilt! Free of unproductive thoughts and actions!

On this glorious day that you have allowed me to see, I am divinely determined and dutifully dedicated to live the life you have created for me.

A life of love, peace, joy, fulfillment, and creative activity.

This is the day, God!

Your day! My day!

And for this day, I am so very, very grateful.

And So It Is!

AND THIS IS IT!

A MEANTIME THOUGHT

you have come a mighty long way! It is my prayer that you have learned a lot and grown a lot. It is also my prayer that you will reread, review, redo, and recommit yourself, on a moment by moment basis, to apply the insights you have gained on your journey through the *meantime.* What I desire most of all is for you to realize, accept, and understand that no matter where you have been, what you have experienced, or how you feel about any of it, on a moment's notice, if you stretch your hand out into the darkness, the Spirit of life will grab your hand, pull you to itself, embrace you, and whisper gently into your soul, *Welcome Home!*

I pray that you will honor the Beloved every moment of every day for the rest of eternity. I pray that your life will be so full of love that you will breathe more deeply, move more slowly, and give more of yourself to the world. I pray that if you ever again find that you are stuck, or living in the basement, resisting change, or doubting the grace or mercy of your beloved Self, that you will reach your hand out into the darkness to be welcomed home—again. I pray that this effort of love, offered in love, for the sake of love, will be a light unto any darkness that has covered the beauty of your soul. In the *meantime,* please know that you are loved; that there is value in every valley; that if you simply act on faith, you will tap the power within. The power within you, my Beloved, is the presence of God—by all names S/He is known.

Be Blessed!

GLOSSARY

Acceptance

To know that all is well, even when you do not see or understand how it will turn out.

Accountability

Considering all actions as creative energy for which you must answer to a Higher Authority.

Affirmation

A statement made and accepted as truth.

Aggression

Pushing, forcing, moving against the natural, normal, or visible flow.

Alignment

Being in one accord, in harmony and balance with the flow of Divine energy.

Anger

The emotional reaction to not having our way or not having people and events meet our expectations.

Awareness

An inner knowing of Divine principles and how they work or manifest in the physical world.

Balance

Having and making time or spending time and energy attending to all areas and aspects of living/being.

Belief

A mental and emotional acceptance of an idea as being the truth.

Betrayal

When expectations of people and events violate trust given, or when one who is trusted is actively dishonest.

Blame

Giving someone else responsibility for your happiness or well-being. Looking outside of self for the answer or solution.

Blessings

Good fortune which comes your way without any conscious input on your part. The demonstration of God's grace and loving in the physical form.

Celebration

Freedom of the spirit. Giving praise and thanksgiving. Feeling good and demonstrating what you feel.

Change

A shift or movement in the flow of life. The outgrowth of the natural flow of events.

Character

The basic essence of the person. What you psychologically and emotionally rely upon, stand upon, look to, hold on to within your self. The foundation of ability to live.

Commitment

Unwavering focus. Giving of all one has to offer. Dedication to and faith in a desired course of events.

Compassion

The ability to see error without the need to condemn. An open and understanding heart with the ability to offer mercy, truth, and love.

Confinement

Mental, emotional, spiritual, or physical impediments to movement, growth, or evolution. A test of spiritual constitution.

Conflict

Disharmony. Imbalance. Opposition between forces, energy, or people moving in similar or differing directions. A test of character.

Confusion

Mental, emotional, or spiritual darkness. Mental, emotional or spiritual conflict. Overstimulation of physical senses.

Consciousness

The total of all ideas accumulated in the individual mind which affects the present state of being. The composite framework of beliefs, thoughts, emotions, sensations, and knowledge which feeds the conscious, subconscious, and superconscious aspects of the individual mind.

Control

Aggression. Conscious attempts to direct the course of events. Unconscious beliefs which stagnate or stymie the course of events. The ability to adjust to the natural flow of events.

Cooperation

The working of one accord, being in togetherness of two or more forces. Balance, harmony, mutual recognition among forces.

Courage

Freedom from fear. The ability to be, stand, move in the presence of anxiety, danger, opposition. Stepping beyond the mental, emotional, or physical state, the place where one is safe, comfortable or secure. A test of character.

Death

Spiritual transition from one form to another. The absence of life, whether physical, emotional, or spiritual. Physical dissolution of the body or a circumstance.

Denial

Conscious failure or subconscious inability to see, know, or accept truth. As related to affirmations or the spoken word, a denial is the soap and water of the mind which relinquishes a false belief or evil thought.

Depression
Unexpressed anger turned inward; feeling burdened or overwhelmed; powerless in the face of situations, unable to have our way.

Desperation
A belief in physical, emotional, or spiritual abandonment. Actions taken in denial of truth. Resistance to beliefs of helplessness. Failure to surrender. Relinquishing of faith and trust. A test of character.

Detachment
A mental, emotional, and spiritual construct which enables one to withdraw emotional investment in a course of events. The ability to become a witness rather than participant. Having no mental or emotional attachment to outcome.

Disappointment
An emotional construct. Expectations based on false or uncommunicated desires which go unmet. Unfulfilled attachments to outcome of events.

Discernment
"The ability to lay hold of truth." To see beyond appearances to that which is obscure and hidden, but divine.

Discipline
Focus. A test of spiritual constitution. The willingness to be taught. The ability to follow through based on faith and obedience.

Diversion

Action or activity which attracts one's focus or attention. A conscious or unconscious act taken in response to fear which impedes growth and evolution. A test of character and spiritual constitution.

Divine Mind

The absolute. The alpha (beginning) and omega (ending) of creation and life; the unlimited, ever-present, all-knowing, all-powerful Spirit of God.

Doubt

The result of trust and truth being brought into question. Lack of focus and commitment that results in fear. The root of mental and spiritual weakness, leading to indecisiveness. A test of character.

Drama

Active participation in conflict, confusion, and the appearance of that which is false. The attempt to get attention or secure control. Resistance to change. Denial of truth!

Ego

"Easing God Out," seeing our way as the way. Believing we are separate from God. The foundation of fear.

Empathy

The ability to stand in the circumstances of another and know the truth without judgment. To give to another what one desires for one's self.

Endurance

Unwavering strength grounded in truth and spiritual principles. An outgrowth of courage. The reward of surrender. A test of character.

Evolution

The calling to a higher order. Development achieved by adherence to spiritual law. The unfolding of natural events according to the divinely ordained spiritual plan.

Excitement

A lifting or rising up of the consciousness. An expression of good. The prelude to joy. An outgrowth of acceptance.

Faith

Spiritual assurance, inner knowing which draws on the power of the heart's desire. Reliance on God's goodness to deliver you from all harm.

Fear

False Expectations Appearing Real. Dread, alarm, painful emotion enhanced by the belief in separation. The basic tool of the ego to find fault.

Forgiveness

To give up the old for the new, the bad for the good. To allow change to take place. An appeal for healing of the consciousness.

Freedom

A mental construct. The ability to know and live the truth. The ability to choose. A state of being without thought of confinement, restraint, limitation, or oppression; having a sense of well-being within that manifests into the outer world.

Grace The omnipresent, omnipotent, all-knowing, perfecting presence of God.

Gratitude Humility of the spirit, which gives praise for all. The act of giving praise. The willingness to receive. A test of spiritual discernment.

Greed Insatiable appetite of the physical senses. The absence of gratitude. Belief in lack.

Guilt The belief that there is something profoundly wrong with an act we have committed. A toxic emotion which often leads to shame.

Healing Restoration of the mind, body, or spirit to a state of Oneness with God. Belief in openness to, receptivity to the presence of God as Spirit.

Helplessness A mental construct. Failure to recognize truth. Denying the Divine Presence. As it relates to surrender, helplessness is the admission and acceptance of the omnipotence of Spirit.

Honesty

Willingness to know, accept, and promote the truth. The conscious participation in the activation of truth whether or not it is spoken.

Humility

Making room for the Holy Spirit, God's Spirit to express through you. The ability to give and serve without expectations of physical reward. Acknowledging God as the giver and doer of all things.

Illumination

Divinely inspired understanding. The ability to see beyond all physical manifestations to the spiritual principle as an active presence.

Impatience

Fear. The absence of faith. The ego's active deed to be in control of circumstances and people. A test of character.

Innocence

A childlike state of purity. Pure thought. The outgrowth of forgiveness. The eternal state of spirit.

Inspiration

Divine motivation from within.

Instinct (6th Sense)

The voice of Spirit within the consciousness. The presence of the Holy Spirit within the being. (See: Intuition)

Intent

The stated or unstated expectation. The cause of all results. The subconscious motivation of all action.

Intuition

"Teaching from within." The subconscious and superconscious aspect of the individual mind which brings forth information required for spiritual evolution.

Jealousy

Fear. Belief in lack. Manifestation of the lack of self-value, self-worth, and self-love. The ego's need to believe "I'm not good enough" or "I don't deserve."

Joy

The natural expression of the Holy Spirit. A state of well-being and Oneness.

Judgment

Fear. A mental construct which involves evaluation by comparison or contrast. The active manifestation of the need to be right. The inability to discern truth.

Justice

The effects of spiritual cause. Thought and emotion are the cause of all physical realities. What has been sown in thought and feeling that is reaped through experiences.

Knowledge

The scope of information gathered through exposure, experience, and perception. Acquaintance with fact which may or may not be fully reflective of truth. Intellectual knowledge is born of individual mind and subject to judgment. Spiritual knowledge is born of Divine Mind, founded in principle, based on eternal truth.

Lack

Fear. A mental and emotional construct. Denial of Divine Presence. The absence of truth.

Limitation

A mental construct which gives power to people and conditions. Ignorance of the truth. Relinquishing of free choice and free will. An outgrowth of drama.

Loneliness

A mental and emotional construct based on the ego's belief in separation and imperfection. Ignorance of stillness, silence, and/or solitude. A test of spiritual constitution.

Love

In its higher sense, this is the nature of reality: God is Love. Love is of God. Creates harmony, clarity and brings about transformation and unity.
In its lesser sense, it is an emotional attachment one has for or shares with another. It comes and goes, depending on one's mood or attitude.

Meditation

The conscious act of stilling the physical mind. Placing attention on inner communion. Listening within for the voice of Spirit. Cessation of all outward movement and activity.

Mistakes

A natural outgrowth of spiritual evolution. Confusion between knowledge and truth. An act of fear based on false perceptions.

Nonresistance

Willingness to acknowledge and honor the natural flow of events. Relinquishing fear, resentment, and judgment. Fearlessness with a foundation in trust. The prelude to surrender. A test of character and spiritual readiness.

Obedience

Unwavering acknowledgment of Spirit. Trust and honoring of self. An outgrowth of discipline. A test of character.

Obstacle

The appearance or manifestation of mental or physical blocks created by one's own thoughts, beliefs, or actions.

Order

The way of the universe. The system of truth by which all things must occur to create harmony.

Panic

The inevitable outgrowth of disorder and impatience.

216

Patience	Inner calm in the midst of outer chaos. An act of total surrender to divine order.
Peace	Absolute harmony on all levels, mental, physical, emotional, and spiritual. Unconditional love for all things.
Perseverance	To strive to find truth, which brings peace, harmony, and acceptance.
Persistence	Spiritual quality that pushes one on to accomplishment or achievement.
Personal Lies	That which we affirm to ourselves about ourselves and which serves to create belief in lack, restriction, and limitation. A defense mechanism against fear.
Personality	The physical and mental attributes developed in response to environment, experiences, conditioning, and judgments about the same.
Power	The ability to do.
Praise	Thanksgiving. Conscious acknowledgment and acceptance of the Divine Presence.

Prayer	Communication with and consciousness of the Divine Presence within the being. The act of communication with the Divine Presence.
Procrastination	The act of delaying what one is intuitively afraid to know or experience. A mental and physical defense mechanism against conscious and unconscious fears.
Reality	That which is unchanging and eternal. Spiritual presence is in back of all real existence, all that is external is an outgrowth of this presence.
Reflection	The sum of our thought patterns, beliefs, and actions made manifest in our life, world, and affairs.
Respect	Conscious regard or consideration for the physical, mental, emotional, and spiritual presence in our world.
Responsibility	To be accountable for all that exists and occurs in our lives.
Self-Acceptance	Self-knowledge void of criticism and judgment.
Self-Doubt	Second-guessing intuitive knowledge. A reflection of low self-worth and self-esteem.

Self-Esteem

Healthy regard for and beliefs about the self and the ability of self. Self relating to the inner Divinity.

Self-Love

Acceptance of all that we are.

Self-Value

A high level of regard for self and the desires of the heart. The ability to make the well-being of self a priority in all activities. Divine knowledge of self.

Self-Worth

The composite recognition of high self-acceptance and self-esteem. The ability to expect the highest for self and to give the highest of self in all affairs. Recognition of excellence within self.

Shame

The belief that there is something intrinsically wrong with who you are. A toxic emotion growing out of programming, conditioning, environment, and guilt.

Stillness

See: Peace

Surrender

Psychological and emotional release. Acknowledgment of the power of spiritual activity. Obedience to spiritual principle, which evolves into an experience of peace and well-being. An act of acceptance.

Trust Unquestioning belief and fearless expectation in the operation of divine law and order. Mental and emotional commitment to the will of God.

Truth An aspect of God that is absolute and all-encompassing. The foundation of spiritual principle. That which is in accord with Divine principle of God as the creative source and cause. The immutable, everlasting word that is now, has been, will ever be eternally consistent.

Understanding Comprehension of truth and spiritual principle. Integration of intellectual and spiritual knowledge.

Wisdom Intuitive knowing and spiritual intuition. The voice of God within the being as the source of understanding and action. The ability to act in accordance with knowledge and principle.

This glossary was excerpted from
Faith in the Valley
Lessons for Women on the Journey to Peace
by Iyanla Vanzant

INNER VISIONS INSTITUTE FOR
SPIRITUAL DEVELOPMENT

♥

spiritual life coach certification program

We invite you to become a student in our comprehensive and innovative program designed to prepare you to enter today's fastest growing career market. Lecture, demonstration, and participation help our students learn by doing. The two-year basic course provides you with the skills and develops a balanced, integrative process that enables you to make positive and creative changes in your own life. The third year of the program prepares you for an exciting career as a coach in which you can support others in creating the life they desire in any field.

The Inner Visions Institute for Spiritual Development was established in 1988 by bestselling author Iyanla Vanzant. Throughout her career, she has earned a reputation as a powerful and dynamic workshop leader and facilitator. The Spiritual Life Coach Certification Program was established in 1999. The goal of the program was to provide former workshop participants with a more practical, long-term approach to spiritual study. The inaugural class attracted only twenty workshop graduates. The remaining students came from all walks of life and all corners of the world, demonstrating the need for an institution that offers a comprehensive approach to spiritual study. It is the vision of the institute to provide training that can be used to support others who have not been able to avail themselves of the program's offerings. Coaching is the viable medium.

Classes for all three years of the Institute's curriculum meet one weekend per month for nine months and for one week during the month of July or August, depending on your level of study. For a formal application or additional information visit our Web site at:

Innervisions@Innervisionsworldwide.com

Or, write to: Inner Visions Institute for Spiritual Development

926 Philadelphia Avenue

Silver Spring, MD 20910

(301) 608-8750

(301) 608-3813 Fax

Be sure to ask about our Network Membership and receive a complimentary newsletter!

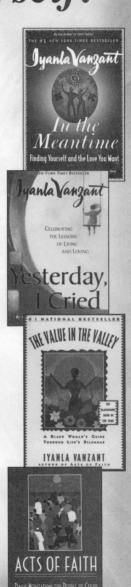